I0105565

لا خنةتحت ؤدام الأمهات

# Paradise Under The Feet of Mothers

A Discourse on the Role &
Reward of Mothers

حسهورش ع باباالواعظ

*Hussein Yushau BabalWaiz*

Copyright © Year 2025

All Rights Reserved by **Hussein Yushau BabalWaiz.**

No part of this publication may be reproduced in any form, or by any means, electronic or mechanical, including photocopying, recording, or any information browsing, storage, or retrieval system, without permission in writing from Hussein Yushau BabalWaiz.

ISBN
Hardcover: 978-1-967616-14-5
Paperback: 978-1-967616-13-8

*Author of "Not good without God" & "Islam Promotes Tolerance and Prohibits Terrorism"*

# Dedication

This book is dedicated to my mother, my grandmothers and to all mothers from Eve to the last mother on planet earth!!!

# Praise & Endorsements

"This book is comprehensive in its scope and exhaustive in content, this book not only inspires but also rewards anyone who reads it."
—Dr. Raji Ayinla, FCCP, FAAC
Director, Bronx Islamic Cultural Center & Professor of Internal Medicine, Columbia University

"An excellent scholarly work, both spiritually and emotionally moving. The Quranic injunctions on fetal development greatly strengthen one's faith in Allah the Almighty."
—Dr. Fusaini Fawzi Mohammed
Family Medicine, Chief of Medicine, Physician Regional Hospital, Naples, Florida

"If words could encapsulate the essence of grace, compassion, and mercy for our parents, then this book has indeed achieved it. Every household should include this masterpiece on its bookshelf."
—Sheikh Ahmed M. Awal
Comparative Religion Scholar & Director, Zaitun Dawah Institute, Seattle, Washington

"I have carefully reviewed *Paradise Under the Feet of Mothers* and found it well written, instructive, and captivating. It contains vital information for students at every academic level."
—Sheikh Abdullahi Gambo
Chief Imam of Yankasa Association & Islamic Studies Instructor, Andalusia High School, Yonkers, New York

"This work will surely benefit the entire Muslim community, especially in societies where raising a family takes extra love and effort. May Allah bless Brother Hussein for writing this book."

—Sister Suwaiba Braimah
Registered Nurse (BSN), Jersey City, New Jersey

---

الْحَمْدُ لِلَّهِ نَحْمَدُهُ وَنَسْتَعِينُهُ وَنَسْتَغْفِرُهُ وَنَعُوذُ بِاللَّهِ مِنْ شُرُورِ أَنْفُسِنَا وَمِنْ سَيِّئَاتِ أَعْمَالِنَا مَنْ يَهْدَهِ اللَّهُ فَلَا مُضِلَّ لَهُ وَمَنْ يُضْلِلْ فَلَا هَادِيَ لَهُ وَأَشْهَدُ أَنْ لَا إِلَهَ إِلَّا اللَّهُ وَحْدَهُ لَا شَرِيكَ لَهُ وَأَنَّ مُحَمَّدًا صَلَّى اللَّهُ عَلَيْهِ وَسَلَّمَ عَبْدُهُ وَرَسُولُهُ

قَالَ اللَّهُ تَعَالَى يَا أَيُّهَا الَّذِينَ آمَنُوا اتَّقُوا اللَّهَ حَقَّ تُقَاتِهِ وَلَا تَمُوتُنَّ إِلَّا وَأَنْتُمْ مُسْلِمُونَ

قَالَ اللَّهُ وَاتَّقُوا اللَّهَ الَّذِي تَسَاءَلُونَ بِهِ وَالْأَرْحَامَ إِنَّ اللَّهَ كَانَ عَلَيْكُمْ رَقِيبًا

قَالَ اللَّهُ اتَّقُوا اللَّهَ وَقُولُوا قَوْلًا سَدِيدًا يُصْلِحْ لَكُمْ أَعْمَالَكُمْ وَيَغْفِرْ لَكُمْ ذُنُوبَكُمْ وَمَنْ يُطِعِ اللَّهَ وَرَسُولَهُ فَقَدْ فَازَ فَوْزًا عَظِيمًا

إِنَّ أَصْدَقَ الْحَدِيثِ كِتَابُ اللَّهِ وَأَحْسَنَ الْهَدْيِ هَدْيُ مُحَمَّدٍ صَلَّى اللَّهُ عَلَيْهِ وَسَلَّمَ وَشَرُّ الْأُمُورِ مُحْدَثَاتُهَا وَكُلُّ مُحْدَثَةٍ بِدْعَةٌ وَكُلُّ بِدْعَةٍ ضَلَالَةٌ وَكُلُّ ضَلَالَةٍ فِي النَّارِ

In the name of Allah, the Gracious, the Merciful

All praise is due to Allah. We praise him, we seek His help, we seek His forgiveness, and we seek refuge in Allah from the evil within ourselves and our evil deeds. Whoever Allah guides, there is none to misguide him. Whoever Allah leads astray, there is none to guide him. I testify there is no God but Allah alone, without any partners, and that Muhammad, peace and blessings be upon him, is His servant and His messenger.

Allah Almighty said, "O you who have faith, fear Allah as it is His right to be feared and do not die unless you are Muslims," (3:102)

And Allah Almighty said, "Fear Allah, from whom you ask each other, and in your family ties, for Allah is ever watchful over you," (4:1)

And Allah Almighty said, "Fear Allah and speak words as befitting. He will amend your deeds for you and forgive your sins. Whoever obeys Allah and His messenger has achieved a great triumph." (33:70-71)

The truest word is the Book of Allah, and the best guidance is the guidance of Muhammad. The most evil matters are those that are newly invented, for every newly invented matter is an innovation. Every innovation is misguidance, and every misguidance is in the Hellfire.

# Contents

# Comments And Commendations About The Book By Some Scholars, Intellectuals And Professionals

*"The book is comprehensive in its scope and exhaustive in its content. I am sure that readers will not only enjoy reading this book, they will also find it most inspiring and rewarding."*

~ Dr. Raji Ayinla, FCCP, FAAC, Director, Bronx Islamic Cultural Center & Professor of Internal Medicine at Columbia University and Head of Residency (Intern doctors) at Harlem Hospital in New York

*"An excellent scholarly work, spiritually and emotionally very moving. The Quran injunctions regarding the development of the fetus does strengthen one's believe in Allah the Al-mighty."*

~ Dr. Fusaini Fawzi Mohammed, Family Medicine. Chief of Medicine, Physician Regional Hospital, Naples, Florida

*"If words could encapsulate the essence of grace, compassion and mercy, in tribute to our parents, then this book have achieved that leverage. I have read the book, and far from exaggeration, Brother Babal-Waiz have somewhat think the thought that most Muslims living in the United States would have wish for a book of this magnitude to be written ,and not just for the benefit of young Muslims, parents also need to read this book and relish it. I recommend every house hold should include this masterpiece in their shelf."*

~ Sheikh Ahmed M Awal, a Muslim Scholar on Science & Comparative Religion, Founder & Director, ZAITUN DAWAH INSTITUTE, Seattle, Washington State

*"I have carefully reviewed the book, "Paradise under Mother's Feet" and found it well written, educative and fascinating with vital information students of various academic levels might need."*

~ Sheikh Abdullahi Gambo, Chief Imam of Yankasa Association & Tutor in Islamic Studies at Andalusia High School Yonkers, New York

*"I believe that this book will be beneficial to all of the Ummah(community) here and back home, but especially here in the United States where raising a family takes extra effort and extra love. I am very proud of you Bro. Hussein for writing this book. May Allah bless you and may He make this the beginning of many more things to come, Amen."*

~ Sister Suwaiba Braimah, A Registered Nurse, BSN, Jersey City, New Jersey

# Acknowledgement

To the Almighty (Allah) God be the glory and gratitude for giving me the strength and wisdom, which has enabled me to delve into in-depth research and write this book, which I have never expected it to attract reviews by a New York Beacon and a Meccan Magazine.

I would not forget to mention the review effort of personalities such Dr. Raji Ayinla of Columbia University Medical School, Dr. Fussaini Fauzi Muhammed of Florida Regional Hospital, Sheikh Ahmed Muhammad Awal of Zaitun Da'awah Institute, Sheikh Baba Gambo, Islamic school teacher and a chaplain, as well as Sister Suwaibah Braimah. They have patiently read and reviewed the book and wrote words of commendation encouraging people to read it.

I also extend my deepest gratitude to brother Abdul Aziz Bilal Abbas, one of my former students, for his invaluable assistance in sub-editing this work. His dedication, expertise, and attention to details have been instrumental in refining this project, and I am truly grateful for his contributions.

# New York
# Beacon

website:
NewYorkBeacon.net

Showing the Way to Truth and Justice

E-Mail
newyorkbeacon@yahoo.com

# New book emphasize[s] importance of mothers

**By Yusef Salaam**

"Paradise under Mothers' Feet" by H.Y. Babal-Waiz is vitally important because it explores the life-giving roles of moms in society, the reward for honoring them, and the penalty for dishonoring them.

The author emphasizes that mothers are the foundation of civilization. They are created with gifts of love, care, compassion, sympathy, and empathy for children. Moms have the awesome responsibility of being the first teachers, and role-models, for children, the future of the world. But, their status has been dangerously lowered in too many places in the world.

Babal-Waiz reports that over a million grandmothers are abused by their own children. In America, many mothers are put in nursing homes. Many are placed there by loving, accountable children, but many "stable" their moms in elderly institutions and don't visit and seldom call them. In America and other countries, adolescents gain authority over their mothers and parents with threats of calling the police and child abuse agencies even when parents are not engaged in abusive behavior.

While the author does not mention it, the most common manner in which American men denigrate moms is their habitual use of the profanity, "motherf......" Another manner that young men disgrace themselves and their moms is when they play the game, "The Dozens," in which they talk about each other's mom in the filthiest sexually perverted mode.

The author uses numerous passages from the Holy Qur'an, the sayings of Prophet Muhammad Ibn Abdullah, and citations of various people, secular and religious, to remind readers of the stellar position of mothers.

Babal-Waiz discusses the natural physical guardian characteristic of moms during pregnancy, "The fetus is protected in the mother's womb like a king in a castle. It is firmly fixed and gets the protection of the mother's body, which it depends on for its growth until birth." During the nine-month ordeal, mothers, who are commonly scorned as "bitches" by men and women, suffer "physically, physiologically, and psychologically in her body due to hormonal changes, leading to nausea, vomiting, fatigue, bloating, flatulence (passing ... quent urine ... and year makes. This ...

(NNPA) ...

... moms give birth. The writer notes that approximately one in ten mothers experience postal-natal depression. Many women suffer various mental maladies "from mild depression, anxiety and post-natal trauma stress to psychotic disorders, including bipolar disorder and schizophrenia." It is no wonder that the Bible promises longevity for one who honors his/her mother and father, notice that mom is cited first.

As far as the primary parent to respect, Prophet Muhammad was asked by an inquirer threes times, which parent to honor. He was seeking an order to rank his closest relatives.

And in that steel-clad male-dominated Arab society, the prophet ranked mothers first, second, and third, and fathers fourth.

Babal-Waiz, a native of Ghana, West Africa, relates the years of nurturing a mother provides a child; breast feeding serves as a special source of food that cow milk and corporate-invented baby food cannot imitate. Women who breast feed do not have the cosmetic concern about what their breast will look like post-breast feeding as too many shallow women do. They want the best for their new born. Moms nurse their children and husbands when they are sick, and they are unable have peace of mind until they are well.

The writer reminds us that no love can match a mom's love, whether human or a mother bear. No matter how loving a wife is to her husband or vice versa, one cannot give the other the quality of love that each received from mom.

Babal-Waiz offers this quote by Abraham Lincoln to accentuate the significance of mothers: "I am indebted with all that she provided to me and I vow to dedicate all that I achieve to my mother exclusively."

Vernon Jordan, advisor to various US presidents, declares: "There will never be a pillow in this world more comfortable and convenient than the lap of mothers." Elizabeth Stone's comment stirs the soul: "Making the decision to have a child is momentous. It is to decide forever to have your heart go walking around outside of your body."

"Paradise under Mothers' Feet" should be welcomed by all. It is priceless at a time when the moral stock index in the world has plummeted as indicated by the critical hemorrhaging of reverence for mothers, women in general, and family life; a time when human values threaten ... level of beasts.several locations un... cases, afreadours of the morning. book is a callus held both a collective naturèse and individual expectartificial. If what this presidency doped ìmean for us,

NEW YORK BEACON, November 18, 2009
newyorkbeacon.net

# THE MUSLIM WORLD LEAGUE
## Journal

The New Islamophobia in France

vol.46    Dhul-Qadah1439/August 2018    No.11

SG of MWL wins Galileo Int. Award 2018

MWL welcomes truce between Afghani government and Taliban

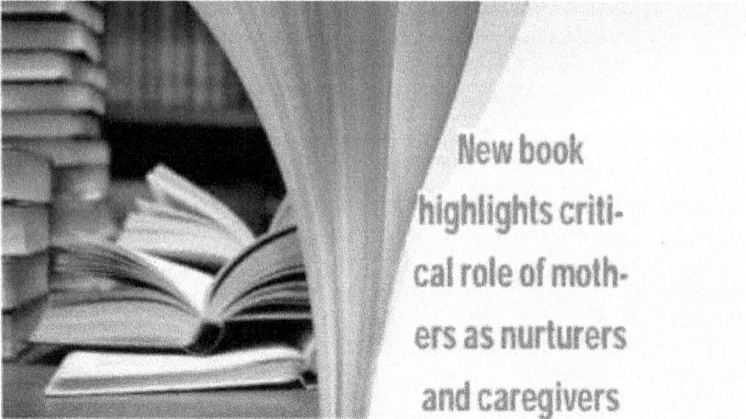

New book highlights critical role of mothers as nurturers and caregivers

**Yusef Salam**

"Paradise is Under Mother's Feet" by H.Y. BabalWaiz, a native of Ghana, West Africa, portrays the life-giving roles of mothers in society, the reward for honoring them, and the penalty for dishonoring them. The author stresses that mothers constitute the foundation of civilization and possess innate qualities of motherhood such as love, care, compassion, sympathy and empathy for children. They have the awesome responsibility of being the first teacher and role model for children, who are the future of the world. However, the status of mothers, the author writes, has been dangerously lowered in many places around the world.

BabalWaiz writes that many sons and daughters put their mothers in nursing homes and seldom visit them, and in some cases they do not visit at all. Laws applicable in some parts of the world permit a son or daughter to gain authority over their parents and even threaten to call the police or child protection agencies on their parents, even if parents have not engaged in any abusive practices.

The author mentions numerous verses of the Holy Qur'an as well as texts of the Hadith, and quotations of secular and religious figures to remind readers of the stellar position of mothers.

BabalWaiz discusses how a mother's womb guards and protects a fetus and how mothers act like guardians of their babies. "The fetus I protected in the mother's womb like a king in a castle."

The fetus is secure and well-protected inside the womb and its development relies heavily on his mother's body until it comes to this world. The author writes "During the nine-month ordeal... mothers suffer physically, physiologically and psychologically due to hormonal changes, leading to nausea, vomiting, fatigue, bloating, flatulence (passing gas), frequent urination and mood swings."

A man approached Prophet Muhammad (peace be upon him) and asked him three times whom of the parents should be honored. The Prophet, answered "your mother" three times to highlight the importance of mothers over fathers. He said "your father" once.

BabalWaiz highlights the importance of breastfeeding, describing it as the richest source of nutrition, which is better for infants than cow's milk or any baby formula.

Breastfeeding mothers want the best for their newborn. Moreover, it is mothers who nurse their children and husbands when they are sick. Mothers won't have peace of mind until they see their children and husbands feeling well.

The writer reminds us that no love can match a mother's love. No matter how loving a wife is to her husband or vice versa, no husband or child will be able to give mothers or wives the same quality of love.

BabalWaiz offers this quote by Abraham Lincoln to accentuate the significant role of mothers: "I am indebted with all that she provided to me and I vow to dedicate all that I achieve to my mother exclusively."

Vernon Jordan, the advisor to various U.S. Presidents, declares: "There will never be a pillow in this world more comfortable and convenient than the lap of mothers". Elizabeth Stone's comment is soul-stirring: "Making the decision to have a child is momentous. It is to decide forever to have your heart go walking around outside of your body."

"Paradise is under Mother's Feet" should be welcomed by all. It is priceless at a time when the moral stock index in the world has plummeted; a time when human values threaten to stoop to the lowest levels. And in innumerable cases, they already have. BabalWaiz's book is a call for us to return to our true nature.

7

# Introduction

Since the inception of creation, which Allah initiated with Adam and created our grand Mother Hawwa' or Eve (in the biblical context) from his ribs, Allah made mothers our main source of life. They delivered and nurtured the prophets, the great *sahabah*, the *taabi'een* (the second generation of Muslims), and the legendary men that had transformed the socio-cultural, political, spiritual, economic and scientific landscape of the entire world. Inherently blessed with boundless love, care, empathy, and compassion, mothers exhibit qualities that seldom manifest so powerfully in men. By His wisdom, Allah the Most Merciful embedded these special traits in women, making them naturally inclined to protect and nurture their children. These out-standing qualities of mothers do not manifest in their opposite gender, because Allah the Al-Mighty, the Ever Compassionate, the Omnipotent, the Omnipresent exclusively embedded this involuntary system into women.

### Religion as a Bond of Love

According to Dr. Aminah Bilal Philips in his book, تفسير أصول (Methodology of Quranic Interpretation), religion comes from the Latin root word *religare*, meaning "to bind." Similarly, *ad-deen* is said by some Arabic grammarians and Quranic interpreters to derive from *ad-dayn*, which means "debt." *Ad-deen* therefore means the repaying of your dept to God. The process consists of our entire day to day life and one of the most important forms of this debt that we have to pay to Allah indirectly should be paid directly to our parents, especially mothers who are the main source of our existence on this earth.

Hence Islam, being a complete way of llif has strongly advocated obedience to parents in various specific Qur'anic injunctions and authentic *Ahadith* (traditions) of the Holy Prophet Muhammad (S.A.W.).

Even the secular societies appreciate the tremendous role mothers play in the life of mankind. No wonder the U.S. and several other countries celebrate Mothers' Day on the second Sunday in May of every year. This holiday was initiated as early as 1900s by Anna Chaves, who began a campaign to honor mothers in America. She spoke with friends and friends of friends. She wrote to congressmen, local leaders, teachers and newspaper publishers. Finally, President Wilson signed a resolution in May of 1914 that officially established Mothers' Day. Anna Chaves thought mothers should be honored with expressions of love and respect. However, despite the effort they put in place and the huge sacrifices they made and are still making while nurturing and raising their kids, there were—and still are—a thousand and one cases or instances of disobedience, disrespect, and abuse towards them. Even secular societies honor mothers. In the United States, Mother's Day occurs every year, yet innumerable cases of maternal neglect and abuse still surface. Many are placed in nursing homes and rarely visited; in some cases, children even call the police on parents who correct them. The moral breakdown in modern societies warrants a renewed emphasis on serving and respecting parents—particularly mothers. President Barack Obama even lamented in his New York Times bestseller, *Audacity of Hope*, that "...raising kids with the right values ranked first in a recent survey conducted(to identify the most pressing problems) in America." According to the BBC Radio Magazine program entitled, *Caring for the Elderly*, which was moderated by Stephen Nolam in June 2007, about a quarter of a million elderly throughout the United Kingdom are being abused by their own children and there are far more than this figure suffering elsewhere in this world.

In the United States, many people move their parents to nursing homes to be taken care of by homecare attendants and many are the instances of abuse, maltreatment and molestation meted out to them by these home health aides. Most of these people do not visit or even call them; they think they have nothing to benefit from them. Dozens of cases have been reported in the U.S. where children would call 911 or the police for their parents for the "crime" of correcting or disciplining them to be good and cultured individuals in the future. As a result, it is no surprise that the youth in America have the gut to put up a program on a television network that serves as a forum for several young guys to appear who are willing to talk in a very derogatory, insulting and sexually perverted manner about each other's mothers without feeling ashamed of themselves or feeling shy of the on-looking audience.

It is upon these various incidents of violation, disobedience, disrespect and abuse towards parents that I attempt this in-depth research to refresh the mind of the youth and the up-and-coming generation about their duties, roles and responsibilities toward their parents—especially mothers—as was sanctioned by the Qu'ran and the Sunnah of the Prophet Muhammad (S.A.W.). This book seeks to remind our youth (and future generations) of the duties and responsibilities enjoined by the Quran and the Prophetic traditions (Sunnah).

I therefore pray to Allah, the All-Mighty to enable the youth in particular to read and reflect soberly and thereby pay heed to the various advice offered by the Qur'anic injunctions and the *Ahadith* that touched on the merits and demerits of parental obedience and disobedience respectively. May Allah grant us the ability to read, reflect, and implement the teachings highlighted herein, securing success in this life and the eternal Hereafter.

M     O     T     H     E     R

{Mercy} {Old} {Tears} {Heart} {Eyes} {Right}


[M]---is for the mercy in millions that she gives.

[O]----means only that she's growing old.

[T]----is for the tears she shed to save me.

[H]----is for her heart of purest gold.

[E]---- is for her eyes with love-light shining.

[R]----means right, and right she will always be.


*Put them all together, they spell "MOTHER",*
*a word that means the world to me.*
---Howard Johnson (1915)

# My Miracle Mother

*Mom, I look at you, and see a walking miracle*

*Your unfailing Love without limit,*

*Your ability to soothe my every hurt,*

*The way you are on duty, unselfishly,*

*Every hour every day,*

*Makes me so grateful.*

*That I am yours and you are mine.*

*With open arms and open heart,*

*With enduring patience and inner strength,*

*You gave so much for me,*

*Sometimes at your expense.*

*You are my teacher, my comforter, my encourager,*

*appreciating all, forgiving all.*

*Sometimes I took you for granted Mom,*

*But I don't now, and I never will again.*

*My miracle, my mother.*

—Joanna Fuchs.

*"Making the decision to have a child is momentous. It is to decide for ever to have your heart go walking around outside your body."*

--- Elizabeth Stone

# Chapter One

## The Miracle Of Creation, Pregnancy & Childbirth

*"Before you were conceived I wanted you*
*Before you were born I loved you*
*Before you were here an hour I would die for you1*
*This is the miracle of Life."*

—Mauree Hawkins

A miracle is an extra-ordinary, uncanny, mysterious and unique phenomenon that is exclusively confined to Allah and He alone owns the discretional powers to perform this miracle.

Allah utilized four different methodologies in his human creation: the prime creature, father of mankind, Adam was created without mother and father from clay (earth);his wife, Hawah (Eve), was created from him without a mother; Jesus was also created without a father; and the rest of mankind were all created and are still being created from mothers and fathers.

The Quran (Surat al-Mu'minun, 23:12–14) describes how Allah transforms a seed of sperm into a clot of blood, then a lump of flesh, gradually building bones and covering them with flesh. In an authentic Hadith, the Prophet Muhammad (S.A.W) him says the embryo develops in forty-day stages before the angel of life breathes the spirit into it.

Modern science confirms these remarkable steps—zygote formation, embryonic development, organ growth—showcasing the divine artistry of the Creator. Throughout, mothers endure extreme physical and emotional challenges: nausea, vomiting, mood swings, and the ordeal of labor pains. Yet Allah eases their trials with inborn resilience and a merciful hormonal system.

Scientists revealed that the earth is made up of eight different elements of minerals some of which are iron, copper, calcium and magnesium. All these elements are found in the human body. According to Imam Ahmed Bun Hanbal, on the Authority of Musa'b, may Allah be pleased with him, who narrated from the Prophet (S.A.W) who said, "Allah created Adam from a collection of sand, scooped from the entire earth. Then all children of them [with skin pigmentations similar to the various colors that constitute the soil topography of the entire earth]. Some of them came with white skin, some with black skin and some with red skin and so on. Some are bad and some are good. Some are happy and some are sad and so on." In another Hadith narrated by Ibn Abbas, he said he heard a group of companions of the Prophet (S.A.W) report that the Prophet (S.A.W) had said, "Allah the Almighty sent Angel Gabriel on to the earth to collect some sand to him. The earth Prophet (S.A.W) 'I seek refuge from you not to reduce[anything] from me or to make me ugly.' Gabriel then returned [to Allah] without collecting the sand and said to Allah,'Oh Allah! She sought refuge from you and declined to collect her sand.' Allah then sent Angel Mikaael. She also sought refuge from him and he returned and made the same report as did Gabriel. Then Allah finally sent down the Angel of Death. She sought refuge from him and he said, 'I also seek refuge from God to return to him without carrying out his order.' He there and then collected the sand on different plains of the earth: white, black and red. That is why the children of Adam came out with different colors. He then ascended with the sand to the heaven towards the throne of Allah and then the sand became wet and turned into clay." This obviously is an absolute proof that mankind was created from the earth.

A sober reflection on the intricate engineering dynamics that Allah adopted in the process of human formation and reproduction attests to the fact that Allah alone, is the embodiment of perfection who can perform this miracle. This chapter will deal with some of this process at length.

On the issue of creation, Allah, the Al-Mighty elaborated vividly in the Holy Qu'ran in Suratul Mu'minuun (the Believers) chapter 23verses12-14, where He says:

*"We created mankind from a progeny and from clay (epitome of clay) then we placed him as [a drop of] sperm in a place of rest firmly fixed. Then we made the sperm into a clot of a congealed blood; then of that clot we made of (fetus) lumps; then we made out of that lump bones and clothed the bones with flesh: Then we developed out of it a different creature, so glory be to Allah, the best of creators. And after which you would die. And you will be resurrected on the Day of Judgment".*

The Hadith that coincides with this verse was narrated by Abi Abdul Rahman Abdallah Bin Masud may Allah be pleased with him who said: The Prophet (S.A.W) may the peace and blessings of Allah be upon him said:

*"Verily the creation of each one of you is brought together in his mother's womb for forty days in the form of seed (sperm). He would become a leech-like object and after which would be transformed in a congealed blood. And then life would be injected into him and he would be commanded with four matters: His means of livelihood (daily bread), his work, life span and whether he would be happy(successful) or unhappy(rascal). "*

Based on the above verse and the Hadith, a renowned Islamic scholar from Pakistan Abu A'la Al Maududi, in his Qu'ranic Interpretation entitled, *The Meaning of The Quran*, published in Lahore, Pakistan in 1994, observed that the entire process of human creation can be described in three steps:

1. The initiation of creation (that is upon conception of a woman).
2. The formation or perfection (from a clot of blood to a full fledge human body).
3. Bringing to life (where Allah injects life into the body).

The most celebrated 21st century Qu'ranic Interpreter par excellence, Shiekh Muhammad Mutawwalii Sha'raawii, an Egyptian scholar, analyzed in his book entitled :

*Miracle of the Qur'an* that:

(Everyone should) . . . sit and take a few seconds and ponder over what he or she was created from. From a discharged (water)substance, from a cell so minute and microscopic that it could not be seen by the naked eyes . . . But that your originator, Allah the Almighty in the powers vested into himself, formulated these cells in their minute forms to be the basic matter that initiates the very life of mankind after he created Adam and Eve. It would move along its path without any control to do anything by itself. So, when the power of Allah moves it(cell), part of it would create bones, part would form muscles, part would make nerves, part would carve out the mind, (brains)part would craft the lungs, part would formulate the heart and part would create the eyes, tongue, lips, hands, and legs. The rest would finally remain in the baby's body to serve as the source of development or growth from strength to strength after the baby is born. And at the same time, we see that this cell in its most minute form creates millions of things that are made up in the human body including everything the body needs to live. All these [phenomena] show or indicate an absolute engineering skill that is only in the domain of Allah, the Al-Mighty.

We are all created from billions of cells and at the center of each one is the instructions (from Allah) and the blueprint for building our bodies just stored in a form of a chemical called DNA.

The renowned American writer and motivational speaker, Dr. W.W. Dyer, provided an interesting analysis which buttressed the above verse of the Qu'ran and the wisdom of the Prophet (S.A.W) that comes with it. He wrote in his book entitled, *The Power of Intention* that:

There is what some people call a future-pull in DNA that is present at conception in each of us. In the moment of our conception, when an infinitely tiny drop of human protoplasm(a living substance inside the cell, it compose of nucleic acids, proteins, lipids, carbohydrates and inorganic salts) combines with an egg, life in physical form begins and God directs the growth process of our body structures, the shape of our physical features, our development including our aging are intended in that one moment of conception, the sagging (floppy or droopy) skin, the wrinkles and even our death are all there.

## Commentary & Analysis:

Science has established that just within ten days of fertilization, the mother's hormones will begin to show changes in her body, the embryo elongating after two weeks.

Then after four weeks, the embryo begins to formulate eyes and other organs. After five weeks, the nose begins to take shape. At six weeks, the embryo becomes half an inch long and after seven weeks, the embryo can move its hands with clearly defined fingers and its internal organs are visible. The eyes form at eight weeks and the fingers of the hands are well defined at ten weeks. Now the embryo is considered a fetus and can move actively. At eleven weeks, it increases by two and half inches long and at twelve weeks three inches long. By fourteen weeks, it palms are formulated. By fifteen weeks, the sensory organs are nearly completely formed and by seventeen weeks it is actively turning inside the mother's womb. At this time, it begins to make strange sounds—referred to as "fetal respiration"—with its eyes closed, though it can see. It receives food from the mother through the umbilical cord and expels its waste through the same cord. At this stage, all its physiological features are fully developed, but it takes another eight weeks for the fetus to have a remote chance of surviving outside its mother's womb. The growth in this fetal stage is silent and unseen.

The fetus is protected in the mother's womb like a king in a castle; it is firmly fixed and gets the protection of the mother's body on which it depends for its own growth until birth. Believe it or not, in all the above-mentioned processes, the mother feels the impact physically and physiologically due to hormonal changes, leading to nausea, vomiting, fatigue, queasy feeling, bloating, flatulence, frequent urination and mood swings.

Eventually, the fetus is ready to be delivered, the uterus begins its powerful contractions, and the process of birth begins. At this point, the sort of severe pain that mothers undergo is highly unbearable.

Upon delivery, Allah the Merciful and Al-Mighty makes the woman produce chemicals in her body that defuses this pain as a sort of immediate post-natal anaesthesia. This and the joy of a newborn baby placed in her fold would make her resist the pain she underwent and thereby relieve the anxiety associated with the thought of undergoing another reproductive process in the future.

## Post-Natal Pains, Depression and Desperation

According to statistics, half a million mothers die during pregnancy and childbirth each year and four million newborn babies die in the first month of life. In the United Kingdom alone, about 268 of women's death were directly related to pregnancy between 1994 and 1996. According to the world health organization, on the global scale, 1600 women a day die from complications of pregnancy and childbirth, making an annual toll of at least 585,000 deaths. In addition, more than 50 million women suffer from complications which lead to long-term health problems, including infertility and permanent incontinence. Despite excruciating discomfort, mothers continue to love and nurture their children at all costs.

Every year, 100,000 women across the developing world find their lives destroyed by "obstetric fistula," an injury sustained by obstructed labor. They become incontinent and are often ostracized by their community. It was discovered that many mothers and their babies die because of simple things like a lack of certain vitamins or because their labors were too long and they needed medical intervention such as a caesarian section.

Around one in ten mothers suffer from post–natal depression after having a baby. If untreated, it can last for months or sometimes longer. Some mothers could be on anti-depressants for up to six months to avoid excessive feelings of anxiety, guilt, uncertainty, loss of control, or other emotions that refuse to go away.

It is not surprising that fifty percent of women in the western world say they have had some forms of negative feelings about being mothers. A recent poll conducted by the website, net-mums in which women answered questions about how they felt after having a baby, suggests that the condition is far more widespread, affecting about fifty-two percent of women. In most cases, the mother's stress is linked to the baby's allergies.

A survey done by the British Broadcasting Corporation (BBC) suggested that, forty-four percent of post-natal depression cases are being concealed from visitors, because many women fear that their children would be taken away from them if they admitted having the problem. Just imagine (in spite of their anxiety) how they feel for their new born not to fall in the hands of foster mothers, who would not have human feelings and empathy as they naturally have for their babies. The facts and figures further revealed that around one in every seven women experience some type of mental health problem during or after pregnancy, ranging from mild depression, anxiety, and post-traumatic stress to psychotic disorders including bipolar disorder and schizophrenia. This can cause considerable distress for the mother, affecting obstetric outcomes, development of the child and creating tremendous stress, and anxiety for family members.

## Motherhood: A Journey of Pain and Sacrifice

From the moment of conception, a mother's role is one of unparalleled sacrifice. Her journey is marked by discomfort and selflessness, as she prioritizes the life she carries within her over her own. As Sheikh Muhammad Bin Saleh Al-Othaimeen (رَحِمَهُ ٱللَّٰه) poignantly observed: "A child comes out from the father through pleasure and comes out from the mother through pain."

This sacrifice begins with the physical toll of pregnancy and extends into the postpartum period, when sleepless nights and endless worries define a mother's world. Through it all, she prays fervently for her child's well-being, trusting in Allah's wisdom and mercy.

## The Divine Gift of Breastfeeding

Breastfeeding, a divine act designed by Allah (سُبْحَٰنَهُ وَتَعَٰلَىٰ), is more than a source of nourishment; it is a bond that forms the foundation of a child's emotional security. The mother's milk, perfectly tailored to her baby's needs, provides essential nutrients like calcium, iron, and magnesium, while also boosting the child's immune system. Modern science marvels at the adaptability of breast milk, which changes to suit the baby's developmental stages and even adjusts its temperature based on the climate.

An American thinker beautifully captured this transition from womb to world:☐ "In the womb, a child experiences five-star care. When they are born, they cry as if mourning the loss of that luxury—until their mother consoles them with tender care outside the womb."

Breastfeeding is more than a biological function; it is a sacred expression of a mother's devotion, fostering emotional intelligence, security, and a lifelong connection between mother and child.

### The Priceless Role of a Mother

Motherhood is not a role defined by scheduled hours or measurable rewards. It is a lifelong vocation, characterized by tireless sacrifice and boundless love. From soothing her child's cries in the dead of night to celebrating their smallest achievements, a mother gives endlessly.

As Vernon Jordan eloquently stated: "There will never be a pillow in this world more comfortable than the lap of a mother."

Scientific studies further validate this, linking breastfeeding to enhanced intellectual development. A 2008 study in the Archives of General Psychiatry found that children whose mothers breastfed as part of a structured program had IQ scores up to 7.5 points higher than non-breastfed children. As Professor Michael Kramer observed: "Increasing IQ by even a few points across a population can result in fewer children at the low end and more Einsteins at the high end."

Yet, in modern times, breastfeeding has declined, often overshadowed by misconceptions about convenience and appearance. This neglect not only deprives children of physical benefits but also of the profound emotional bond that comes with it.

## A Mother's Endless Devotion

A mother's sacrifices are countless and immeasurable. She endures sleepless nights, prays through tears, and finds joy in her child's happiness. From teaching first words to instilling moral values, a mother shapes her child into a compassionate and resilient member of society.

Islam recognizes this, elevating mothers to an unparalleled status. When the Prophet Muhammad (S.A.W) was asked who deserved the most good treatment, he replied: "Your mother." "Then who?" "Your mother." "Then who?" "Your mother." "Then your father." (Sahih Bukhari, Sahih Muslim)

This repetition underscores the pivotal role of mothers in a child's life.

## Timeless Stories of Maternal Sacrifice

The annals of history are filled with stories of mothers whose love defied all odds. Consider Hajar (Hagar), the mother of Ismail (peace be upon them), who ran between the hills of Safa and Marwah in search of water for her thirsty child. Her act of compassion became an eternal ritual in the Hajj pilgrimage, reminding Muslims of the power of maternal devotion.

Another poignant tale is of a mother who sacrificed one of her eyes to restore her son's sight. Her son only learned of her selflessness on her deathbed, leaving him in awe of her boundless love. Such sacrifices transcend time and culture, proving that a mother's love knows no limits.

## Fatherhood: A Role of Support and Guidance

While the mother's role is unparalleled in its intimacy and sacrifice, the father's contributions are equally vital. Fathers work tirelessly to provide for their families, ensuring their children have access to education and opportunities. They offer guidance, instilling discipline, values, and a strong moral compass.

Theodore Hesburgh once said: "The most important thing a father can do for his children is to love their mother."

A father's love and support not only strengthen the family unit but also create an environment in which children thrive.

### Reflections on Parental Legacy

The legacy of parents—especially mothers—is a profound one. Sayyid Qutb, a prominent Islamic scholar, dedicated his book The Artistic Representation of the Qur'an to his mother, reminiscing about her role in nurturing his love for the Qur'an: "To you, my dear mother, I dedicate this book... You sent me to school with the ambition that I memorize the Qur'an, and you prayed fervently for my success. Your last memory is of sitting by the radio, listening to Qur'anic recitation, your face glowing with understanding and peace. This book is the fruit of your unwavering dedication."

Sayyid's words remind us that a mother's influence shapes her children's lives long after she has passed.

### Conclusion: A Tribute to Mothers

A mother is a school, a garden, and a teacher of unparalleled wisdom. As Ahmad Shawqi poetically wrote: "A mother is a school—prepare her well,☐ And you prepare a people of noble character.☐ A mother is a garden—nurture her, And she will blossom with extraordinary beauty.

The role of parents in nurturing their children transcends generations. Through their sacrifices, wisdom, and love, they shape the leaders, thinkers, and compassionate beings of tomorrow.

## From The Mass Media

According to doctors, a woman is more capable of resisting pains than a man. When asked why that is the case, they said labor pains is enough evidence.

*The theme of the above poem revolves around dishonor and humiliation toward parents. It was composed by a companion, Ubaid-Lah Bin Khalsah, after he came to the Prophet (S.A.W)*

*"Making the decision to have a child is momentous. It is to decide for ever to have your heart go walking around outside your body."*
--- Elizabeth Stone

crying. The Prophet (S.A.W) asked him why he was crying and he said: My son used to be poor and I used to be rich; he used to be weak and I used to be strong. However, when I became poor and he became rich, I became weak and he became strong, he refused to help me with his money. The

Prophet (S.A.W) then sent the man to call his son. Before he and his son reach the Prophet (S.A.W), Allah sent down Angel Gabriel to tell the Prophet (S.A.W) that, when they reach him, he should ask the father what he was reciting in his heart on their way to him. So, upon arrival, the Prophet (S.A.W) did ask him and he said, "By Allah I was talking to my son and reciting this poem that goes as follows:

*I fed you before you were born (through the umbilical cord).*

*When you were in pain I do not sleep.*

*Because of your plight, I remained sleepless turning around,*

*As if I was the one in pain.*

*My heart bleeded in fear of your death.*

*Even though I know that death is matter of time.*

*However when you grew up or you mature,*

*You preferred insult and abusive attitude as my reward,*

*As if you were the one who raised me*

*But woe onto you if you do not recognize my effort in raising you,*

*As a mere neighbor would relate to me.*

*And you truly related to me as a neighbor.*

*Remember I spent my money on you.*

*But you are now refusing to spend on me or being stingy to me.*

Upon reciting this poem, the Prophet (S.A.W) could not hold his tears and pulled the boy closer to him saying, "my son, there is neither a mountain, nor a tree nor a body of rainwater on this earth presently that does not wail and weep for this act of contempt towards your father. Give your father what he asked from your money, for you and your money belong to your father." The above poetic description is what mothers really go through in their effort towards raising children.

A mother is like a tree; all her parts are useful for her children.

A beautiful story entitled, "An Old Tree" which has appeared in several books of oral history and Arabic literature elaborates on this metaphor. It is consist of a boy and an apple tree. The boy would climb up and down, playing on the tree and its branches. When he grew up and began to struggle for life, looking for a means of livelihood, the tree became sad because the boy did not come to her anymore. The boy however paid a visit to the tree after a long absence.

She asked him, "Why did you stop coming to me?"

He said, "I used to play with you when I was young, but now I am a grown person."

She said, "Okay, sit and let's have a chat."

He said, "I can't sit because I need money to solve my problems."

She said, "but I have no money to help you with, so take as many apples as you want from me and go and sell them to make money and use it for your needs."

The boy climbed on the tree and harvested many of the apples, went to the market and sold them. He began to make use of the money. He later matured and was about to get married and wanted to build a house for his family. He came back to the big old tree and told her, "I want to get married, but I don't have materials to build a house for my family."

The tree told him, "You know I have been helping you since you were young, so just cut my branches and use them to build your house."

He cut the branches, gathered them and built his house. A few days later, a heavy windstorm invaded the town and destroyed the building. The man wanted to have something to climb on to walk on the river so he again came to the tree and told her to help him. She said, "This is the only remaining part of me, I gave you all my apples and my branches, so take half of me and build a boat so you can walk on the river."

He cut the tree in half and built a boat with it. Later when he grew old, he came to the tree again and said, "I am now too old and would like your permission to always come to lean on you, in order to take rest and enjoy fresh air." The tree said, "no problem! You are always welcome and I am always here for you."

This tree symbolizes the mother, who always gives to her children, going the extra mile to please them and does not take from them.

*"There is not a relationship in a family that is more important than
the relationship a child has with( his or) her mother."*

—Michelle Obama, First Lady of the United States.

# Chapter Two

## The Role Of Parents In Child Nurturing

*"So when the great word" Mother!" rang once more,*
*I saw at last its meaning and its place;*
*Not the blind passion of the brooding past,*
*But Mother . . . the World's Mother . . . come at last,*
*To love as she had never loved before . . .*
*To feed and guard and teach the human race. "*

— Charlotte Perkins Gilman

A man after getting married to a woman is blessed by Allah when he causes the woman to conceive or become pregnant; his blessing is enhanced even more. According to Ustaz Ahmed Saeed, a Ghanaian scholar, the father feels the impact of his wife's pregnancy physiologically. He experiences a feverish condition and cold symptoms indicating that a drop of his sperm in her womb has started a process of transformation into a human creature like him. However, as the late Sheikh Muhammad Bin Saleh Al-Othaimeen, a renowned Saudi scholar observed, "A child comes out from the father through pleasure and comes out from his mother through pain." Upon conception, she begins to feel unbearable pains, but she places herself in a position of security, comfort and convenience to her offspring. She sacrifices delicacies and any meal that would endanger the development of the child yet unborn.

After delivery, a child is incapable of feeding himself or herself, so she breastfeeds him. It is through breast feeding that the child begins to develop a close relationship with his or her mother. A close observation at a mother breast feeding her baby attests to this fact.

After the baby takes a short break and releases her nipple from his or her mouth, one would see the child smiling at the mother. The child by doing so is expressing his or her appreciation for her care, though non-verbally. Some analysts even say this love begins right from the womb, because he eats from what she eats through the umbilical cord. As an American think tank put it, "If you are in your mother's womb you have a five star [hotel] treatment, a full fledge treatment and as soon as you get separated from her, on the first day of your birth as you come out of her, you cry so hard, thinking you are going to lose that five-star treatment." But your mother relieves you from this fear by her unique treatment out of her womb like a fragile egg.

Upon various interviews with some mothers, it was revealed that when a breast-feeding mother goes out and leaves her baby home, the moment he feels hungry and begins to cry, her nipples start releasing milk simultaneously regardless of the distance between her and the baby. If she feels the drip of her milk, she rushes home to breast-feed her baby. If the baby is content or satisfied, the milk stops flowing. It later begins to flow when the baby feels hungry.

Allah programmed the child since he was in his mother's womb with his sensory organs to be able to know or feel her temperature, so whenever he cries and a different woman takes him on her chest to breastfeed him, he continues to cry because he does not feel the same temperature that he knows his mother with. And interestingly, if the mother comes and puts him on her back, he feels the same as he feels with the strange woman, because he is not familiar with the back temperature, and it is only when she places him on her chest to breast-feed him that he stops crying. *Subhaanallah*! (To God be the glory). Imagine a "magnetic reaction" between a mother and her child in spite of her absence. And whenever the baby cries, it is only the mother's breast that consoles him or her.

The temperature level of the mother's milk is the same as that of the baby's body through the period of breast feeding. Allah created the breast to produce warm milk in winter and cold milk in summer for the baby. In other words, the mother's milk tends to adjust to the seasonal change of weather to provide comfort for the baby. The milk (with water) contains components such as iron, calcium, magnesium and different kinds of vitamins that help in the physical development of the child and help produce strong teeth for him or her and serve as immune system against diseases during infancy.

She always prays to Allah to guide and guard him against all evil. Days and nights go by and she continues to be at the baby's side—twenty-four hours a day, seven days a week. It is not a nine-to-five kind of work, where one punches in and out or swipes in and out, but a round-the-clock job until the child reaches the weaning period.

Breast-feeding is the most priceless gift of love from mother to child that lasts a lifetime. The child inherits a myriad of qualities from the mother during this moment, ranging from compassion to patience. A recent scientific study established that increased breastfeeding by a mother during the first months of life appears to raise a child's verbal intellectual quotient (IQ), according to a study of nearly 14,000 children released on May 5th, 2008 and published on a website called am NY in an article on health. The study in the United States *Archives of General Psychiatry* found that six-year-olds, whose mothers were part of a program that encourages them to breastfeed, had a verbal IQ that was 7.5 points higher than children in a control group. The results echo previous studies that found children and adults who were breastfed tended to have higher 1Qs than those who were not.

Michael Kramer, a professor of pediatrics at McGill University in Montréal, Canada said the IQ improvements were modest and might not be noticeable on an individual basis. But he added that the increase could have a significant effect on society as a whole.

"We're not talking about making a child who has trouble in school and is dropping out into genius," he said. "But if we can increase IQ by three to four points in the whole population, we can have fewer children at the low end and more Einstein's at the high end."

The above analysis presupposes that children who are not breastfed cannot be equated with those breastfed in terms of intellectual capacity, so every child should count himself or herself blessed to have had the chance to enjoy this invaluable "mobile fountain" that their mothers possess, which makes a tremendous impact in the child's physical and mental health. Unfortunately, some mothers in the modern world would prefer to feed their babies with artificial milk to maintain their physical outlook or avoid their breasts "falling flat". It was further revealed that most of the children with deviant behavior were fed with cow's milk when they were babies and that is why they behave like animals without any sympathy and courtesy to their parents. It is no surprise then that this behavior is so common in the western societies where many mothers do not breastfeed children.

A mother is the most priceless treasure that one can ever have on this earth. She twinkles like a morning star and sparkles like a precious diamond and glitters like a golden ornament. She guides against anything no matter how small it is in a bid to protect her baby. Many were instances she spent sleepless nights as a result of pains during the stages of her baby's transformation. Pens are incapable of recording the severity of her struggles. She cried inwardly and outwardly on several occasions and saw herself on the verge of death until this little baby of hers came out of this world.

*"There will never be a pillow in this world more comfortable and convenient than the lap of mothers."*

—Vernon Jordan

So many years have passed when she would carry you on her back or chest, you defecated on her. She washed you with her bare hands and she made a special cradle for you on her bed. Her chest served as your source of food. She appears happy and took delight in doing things that would ensure your well-being. In her heart, beams—and continues to beam—a light of sincere love, sympathy, empathy, affection, and compassion.

She is an embodiment of kindness and consideration. She is like a tree that bears healthy and well nurtured seeds and fruits.

Remember when you fell sick and could not sleep, she spent sleepless nights eager to see you in good shape. She shed tears when you were not responding to treatment till Allah blessed you with full recovery. It was there and then that this wonderful woman would smile and feel comfortable. She would then thank Allah for granting you recovery. She would continue to pray to Him for your protection and prosperity and wish you success in your future endeavors.

She would be dreaming of—and waiting for—your days of adulthood, when it would be your time to get married so as to be happy for you, and at the same time be sad, knowing you would be going to live with a woman like her, but very different from her in sense that no matter how this woman loves and cares for you, you will never feel that unique and extraordinary sense of sincere love, compassion, sympathy and empathy that you were blessed with when you used to be under her care. This is obviously because she feels part and parcel of your flesh and bone—blood is thicker than water, so goes the popular adage.

Any growing child would respond upon questioning that it is his mother that pays more attention towards his education than his father. Mothers mostly attend Parent-Teacher Association (PTA) meetings, including the school's graduation ceremony. There were myriad of instances where some mothers here in America have had sleepless nights because they missed their children who were taken back home by their fathers to Africa and the Arab world to be raised. That unflinching love and affection that they have for their children tells their minds' eyes that they are not in safe hands and are longing to meet them.

In fact, a mother is an everlasting treasure that will soon slip by from those who disrespect and disobey her and an endless treasure for those who respect and obey her. She is like a perfume that leaves its seal uncovered to her child to enjoy the sweet aroma throughout his or her entire life. She was the first person to teach you how to talk and communicate and whenever you cry, she would sing a lullaby to you till you stop crying and begin to smile. She also taught you so many lessons in Islamic code of ethics and social norms and values. She taught you how to relate to people, respect the elderly (especially your father), love your country and sympathize with the weak and the poor. She planted a strong seed of truthfulness in you and urged you to refrain from falsehood and taught you the benefits of trustworthiness when something is entrusted in your care. She did all this for you to enable you to become a well cultured, dynamic, vibrant and vital member of the society.

Above all, a mother has a special place in the sight of Allah as the Prophet Muhammad (S.A.W) told us in the *AHadith* coming up in the chapters ahead. A deviant and disobedient man was forgiven and granted Jannah when his mother prayed for him. A Muslim monk by the name Uyash, a descendant of Basra, narrated that he was once on a visit to one of the suburbs in Iraq when he saw only four Muslims carrying a coffin of a dead person and exclaimed, "Allahu Akbar(God is Great), why should only four people carry a coffin of a dead Muslim to *Janaza* (Funeral Prayer) and the Prophet (S.A.W) said he who prayed on a dead person and escorted the coffin to the burial ground will attract reward as big as the size of two mountains of Uhud in Makkah?" He then followed their footsteps echoing over and over in his mind, "a burial rite that attracted only four people and nobody followed them? This is strange!"

He further narrated that they buried the corpse and after the burial he said to them, "*Subhaanal-Lah*! (Glory be to Allah) what happened to his burial rites? This is unusual." Then one of them told him to ask the only woman among them making her their fifth, claiming that this woman hired only the four guys to bury the corpse for a fee. They prayed over him, carried him to the cemetery, and buried him.

The narrator of this story said he then followed the woman after the burial until he reached her house. He knocked on her door and was permitted to enter. He sat down and started asking her what happened which caused the funeral rites to be attended by a very limited people.

"The deceased was my son," she said. "When he was on the verge of death, he asked me 'Mother, do you wish to see me in happiness and joy in the Hereafter?' I said, 'yes of course, my son.' And frankly speaking, this man used to live a deviant, disobedient, immoral and sinful life and was very disrespectful to me. He continued, '...then Mother, if my death time approaches, recite "*laa ilaaha illal Laah*" to me. And if I die do not inform or invite anybody to my funeral rites because if people know about my sinful acts, they would not pray *Salaatul Janazah* on me. But Mother, raise your hands to Allah and say:

*"Oh, Allah, I hereby declare to you this evening that I am pleased with my son so be pleased with him.' And he asked me to say this prayer three times."*

The woman laughed at this juncture and Uyash, the narrator of the story asked her why she was laughing. She said, "Wallahi (by Allah) I did pray as he asked me to and lo and behold, I heard a strange voice echoing to me after the burial that:

*"My Mom! My Mom! I met my Lord, so Merciful and Generous was [He] to me and [He] was not angry and dissatisfied with me."*

## Impact Of Mother's Sympathy On The Entire Muslim

### Ummah Hajar (Hagar), Mother of Ismail

Hajar(Hagar), the mother of Ishmael, exhibited a high sense of sympathy towards her son when he became thirsty. It all came about when her husband Ibrahim (Abraham) took them from Palestine to a valley in Makkah and left them with insufficient water. After they used it up, her son Ishmael started crying out of thirst. Hajar became so worried and sympathetic. She was confused, running from one point (*Safa*) to another (*Marwah*), searching for water and looking for any sign of human movement or noise to seek for help. She finally could not get any help. So upon this sympathy that she expressed towards the child, Allah caused water to gush out from the earth beneath the toes of Ishmael and thousands of years later this physical effort made by Hajar became part and parcel of the *sunnah* of *Hajj* rituals. Just imagine how motherly sympathy towards her son resulted into an amazing *jihadic* ritual of *Hajj*. The importance of this ritual cannot be questioned because the Prophet (S.A.W) is reported to have said in a long Hadith, stating the various rituals of *Hajj* and the rewards attached to them, he who performs just the ritual of *safa* and *marwah* seven times as Hajar did, his or her reward is equated to someone who has freed seventy slaves.

## A Mother Sacrificed An Eye For The Sake Of Her Son

This mother was tested by Allah with her son losing one of his eyes, as he was growing up. By virtue of that natural motherly love and affection, she decided not to see her son grow up to live with only one eye. She approached an eye surgeon to remove one of her eyes and replace it with her son's deficient eye to enable him to live in comfort and confidence in public. This woman made this incredible sacrifice and lived with one eye for the rest of her life. So when she was on the verge of death, her son who never knew about this incident was by her sick bed. She narrated this sacrificial story to him and he could not hold his tears and amazement for his mother to go the extra-mile to sacrifice the most priceless organ in the human body (that is highly cherished especially by women), just for him to be able to live comfortably. He lamented why she did not inform him about this incident earlier so as to reciprocate this in many ways.

*"I will never feel comfortable unless I am on the laps of my mother."*

—Socrates, Philosopher

# Mother's Advice To Her Daughter On Her Wedding Day

Mothers always go the extra-mile to express their love and affection to their children. History informs us of a pious woman named Umaamatu Bintul-Haris, who isolated herself with her daughter on her wedding night before she was escorted to her husband's home and gave her the following priceless advice:

"Had a woman not had the need of a husband, her parents would have been able to take care of her needs. But women were created for men and men were created for women. So listen to my advice that awakens the slumber. My daughter, my daughter, I love you so much and I am going to miss you so much as you are about to leave the atmosphere that you were raised in and move to a different environment that you are not used to.

You are moving to be in company of your lifelong partner you do not know and are not familiar with for better or for worse, through thick and thin. He will be in charge of your welfare and supervision. So, I implore you to be his servant and he will be a servant to you. Keep and protect these ten life principles and ethics and you will be successful and happy in your marital life with him:

"First and second, you have to be moderate in your request and obedient to his order.

Third and fourth, do not let him see any ugly or nasty sight of you and also do not let him smell any bad odor in you.

Fifth and sixth, make sure you are available to him in bed and serviceable to him in the kitchen.

Seventh and eighth, protect his properties, especially money and take good care of his children and be kind and respectful to his mother.

Ninth and tenth, do not violate his order and do not spread his secret.

Beware of happiness when he is sad and sadness when he is happy.

With this, my daughter, I wish you Allah's protection and blessing in your new world. Wassalaamu Alaik!"

In fact, many mothers since time immemorial gave—and are still giving—these golden principles to their daughters in a bid to ensure success in their new lives with their husbands and wish they could have a behind-the-scenes glimpse of their daughter's marital home to see if they are implementing the letter and spirit of these principles.

*"There is not a relationship in a family that is more important than*
*the relationship a child has with (his or) her mother."*

—Michelle Obama, First Lady of the United States.

## Father's Role In Raising Child

Since you were born, your father took the responsibilities of you and your mother. He would work extra-hard to meet the needs of the family. As you grow up, he sent you to school and paid for your fees to be trained and educated for your future progress. He would always advise and urge you to guide against moral vices and adopt sound moral virtues. He counselled you to be an obedient child, a hardworking and loving student and a well-cultured adult. He indicated to you that all these manners would be contributing factors to your success in life in this world and the hereafter. His ambition was always to see you as the best of all children and it did not bother him to see you achieving higher than what he had achieved.

However, the father himself knows the enormity of the mother's role, which could not be compared with his responsibilities by any stretch of imagination.

*"The most important thing a father can do for his children is to love their mother."*

--- Theodore Hesburgh

## To You My (Sayyid Qutb) Mom That I Dedicate This Book.

You often listened from the back of the "Curtain" in the village to the recitation from people whom you used to invite to recite the Qur'an in our home through the entire period of Ramadan. While I happened to be with you, playing around and making noise, you would give me stern advice to be quite and I would keep mute to listen to the recitation with you and my heart would end up absorbing its melodious music, even if I did not understand its meaning. And when I grew up in front of you, you sent me to the primary school in the village and your prior ambition was for Allah to brighten my mind to enable me memorize the Holy Qur'an, and to bless me with a melodious and sweet-sounding voice, so as to recite it to you always. You then finally changed my route to the new route that I am pursuing now. This was after you attained part of your objectives. I then memorized the Qur'an! However, you have made a journey (of no return) far away from me Oh, and your last personal picture is intact in my imagination or memory is of you always sitting in front of the radio and listening to a beautiful recitation (of the Qur'an). It would show in the features of your magnanimous eyes that you assimilated it in your big heart and understood what was apparent in meaning and what was hidden. So dear mother, over to you the fruit of your prolonged attention towards your young child and your young adult. And even if he had lost its beautiful recitation, perhaps he may not lose its great dynamic wisdom. May Allah bless and protect you and him."

—Your Son, Sayyed Qutb.

*A mother is a school when you prepare her,*

*You prepared a people of good veins (well-cultured).*

*A mother is a garden when it is well irrigated; it produces extra-ordinary and unique leaves.*

*A mother is a teacher among teachers that enriches them (her students) with everlasting legacy.*

"*I never knew the meaning of motherhood until when I was blessed with a boy-child, It was then that I realized that whatever I provided to her will never equate one night that she went sleepless because of me.*"

—Aadil Saalim

# Chapter Three

## Impact Of Mothers in The Life of Some Eminent Scholars

*"And when mothers and grandmothers have more often than not anonymously, handed on the creative spark, the seed to the flowers they themselves never hoped to see . . . or like a sealed letter they could not plainly read."*

— Alice Walker

There are numerous examples of Islamic scholars of the second generation, following the Prophet (S.A.W) and his *sahabah* (followers), whose mothers made huge impact in their lives. For example, three of the four most famous and knowledgeable Imams,ءاهقفلاةعبرلأ ةمئلأ)(The four Imams of Islamic jurisprudence), were single handedly taken care of by their mothers. Mothers are often the uncelebrated architects of greatness, quietly shaping the minds and spirits of those destined to leave an indelible mark on the world. History brims with examples of mothers whose dedication and wisdom have elevated their children to extraordinary heights. In Islamic history, the profound influence of mothers on their children is especially evident in the lives of renowned scholars who shaped the spiritual and intellectual legacy of the Muslim world. We will mention just a few famous among the Islamic scholars. This chapter delves into the lives of these luminaries and the immeasurable role their mothers played in their journeys.

Below is the summary of each one of them and the role their mothers played in their upbringing.

1. Imam Malik Ibn Anas, Imam of the Abode of Migration (إمام دار الهجرة ): He grew up with the zeal to seek knowledge and his mother encouraged him. She recognized his potential early on, nurturing his love for knowledge and spirituality. She bought him new clothing with a hat(*kufi*) fine clothing, a traditional kufi, books and pens just to emulate the great scholars and would always urge him to go to the Masjid in Madinah to attend the lessons being given after prayers. He used to have keen interest in music, his mother gently steered him toward scholarship, instilling discipline and ambition, but the mother did not like it. So, this encouragement of hers made him blazed the trail and become the greatest scholar during his time. He produced a book of AHadith—"موطأ ملك "(the approved)—among others, a revered book of Ahadith, which his student Imam Shafi'ee described as the most accurate book after the Holy Quran." In a Hadith related by Imam Tirmidhi and others, the Prophet (S.A.W) may Allah bless him and grant him peace said;

> "A time will soon come when people will beat their camels in search of knowledge and will not find a man of knowledge more knowledgeable than the man of knowledge of Madinah."

> This prophecy is widely believed to refer to Imam Malik. It was established by Furaj, Ibn Uyayna and others that this Hadith refers to Imam Malik. This shows the impact of his mother's effort and prayers

towards him. as she was instrumental in shaping the man who became the "Scholar of Madinah."

2. Imam Shafi'ee: The Father of Usul al-Fiqh (Principles of Jurisprudence). His father died before he was born, so his mother raised, trained and taught him when he was young. Recognizing the transformative power of education, she enrolled him in a Qur'anic school where he memorized the book of Allah at the age of 7. Then he memorized the " موطأ مالك" the (approved book) of Imam Malik at the age of 10. Three years later, his brilliance led him to study directly under Imam Malik himself, earning his mentor's admiration. Shafi'ee became Malik's student. Imam Malik was highly impressed by his memory and intelligence and he later authored " مُسند الإمام شفلعي" (Musnad [support] of Imam Shafi'ee) and many other books. Over the years, Imam Shafi'ee authored numerous groundbreaking works, including مُسندُ إل مَّهمافعي(The Musnad of Imam Shafi'ee), laying the foundation for Islamic legal theory.

4. Imam Ahmed Bun Hanbal: His mother used to wake him up early in the morning, clean and dress him and then take him to the mosque to pray and allow him to sit and listen to the studies in the *masjid*(mosque) after *fajr*(dawn) prayers. After prayers, she ensured he stayed to learn from the scholars. This has impacted his life and he became one of the best scholars of his time and one of Islam's most respected scholars. He produced a book of Hadith dubbed, " مُسند الإمام أحمد بن حنبل" (Musnad of Imam Ahmad), one of the most comprehensive collections of Ahadith, and other titles. His mother's relentless dedication made this possible, proving the transformative power of a mother's influence.

5. Safyanu-Saurii: He was another galaxy among these intellectuals. His mother was very influential in his life. She once told him: "Safyan, seek knowledge and I will take care of your means of livelihood. My son, if you write ten letters, stop and reflect deeper. If you see your piety, patience, and fear of Allah improving, then you are on a right track. And if you do not see this then what you are learning is harming you and not helping you." This profound advice became the compass for his life. Safyan took heed to his mother's advice and became an outstanding scholar among the men of *zuhd* (eternally and otherwordly minded) in his generation. He rose to prominence as a leading figure in zuhd, inspiring generations of scholars.

6. Imam Muhammad Ismail Al-Bukhari ( إمام المحُدِّين): His father died during infancy and the mother took the entire responsibility of bringing him up. He became blind at a young age. The mother consulted many famous and skilled doctors of his time, but their treatments made no difference. His mother was a pious worshipper and a righteous woman. She cried out for help in the court of Allah, the All-Mighty, for her child and begged for the restoration of his eyesight. At last, "the river of mercy flowed over her", and Allah accepted her invocation. One night she visited Prophet Ibrahim in a dream and he told her that, "Allah has restored the sight of your son because of your intense and beautiful invocations." By morning, Imam Bukhari's eyesight was miraculously restored. In the morning, as Imam Bukhari got up from his bed, glimmers of light reached out into his eyes and he grew up with a

photographic memory such that whenever he reads a book it would be committed into memory at once. He produced a complete book of Hadith dubbed, "صٌحيحالبخاري" (Authentic Book of Bukhari), which is inarguably the most authentic book of Hadith after the "موطأ" (Muwatta) of Imam Malik. His brilliance, fueled by his mother's prayers and sacrifices, left an unparalleled legacy. One of his students had a dream that he saw Imam Malik walking behind Prophet Muhammad (S.A.W) and his footstep fell exactly on the footprint of the Prophet (S.A.W); this obviously shows that he was on the right course.

In addition to those mentioned above, a few more among these people of penetrating intellect who were trained and raised by their mothers were: Abdullah Ibn Kathir (among the scholars of the seven modes of Quran recitations), Imam Tirmidhi and Ibn Majah (AHadith Scholars), Saeed Binil-Musayyid, Umar Bin Abdul Aziz aandImamu Abu Hanifa (Scholars in Islamic Jurisprudence) and finally, Imam Hassanul-Basari and Fudail Bin Iyad, who wrote *Aspects in Wisdom* and ز هد (Abstention).

Ponder over the words of an American motivational speaker, prolific writer andintellectual, Dr.W.W.Dyer who attracts huge audience at his programs in the media outlets by virtue of his charisma and charm. Below is what he wrote regarding his mother in his book, *Yes Mom, You Inspired Me!*:

"…What I meant to say was how can I possibly say good bye to the person who was the first to hold me, the first to feed me and the first to make me feel loved?

From a distance I watched you doing the mundane tasks that to every one else seem so routine. But for me, the tasks you lovingly completed year after year built and reinforced the foundation, the structure that made my world a safe, secure and comfortable place to grow. All that I am and all that I have made along the way would not have occurred without first believing in me. And you were the person who always believed in me.

Now with a family of my own, I am amazed at the number of times I hear your words flow from my mouth. This ventriloquist (a stage actor) phenomenon was at first most irritating, but now warms me as I have come to understand that there is a part of you that will live on in me for ever. When time part us, I pray that you will reach across from the other side to again touch my face and whisper into my ear for your warm and gentle presence in my life.... for this, I will always be most thankful...yes, mother you inspired me!"

No matter where Dr. touc spoke, electricity filled the air. Dr. Dyer's dramatic cadence, piercing and penetrating voice was like a baby's lullaby and you could not resist his call for sober reflection.

*"Allah Al-mighty made forbidden for you violation of the rights of mothers and burial of infant girls alive."*

Al-Hadith

*"I never knew the meaning of motherhood until when I was blessed with a boy-child, It was then that I realized that whatever I provided to her will never equate one night that she went sleepless because of me."*

—Aadil Saalim

## Parental Obedience Is An "Advance Loan"

*Be obedient to Allah as He sanctioned*

*And fill your heart with caution*

*Be obedient also to your father for he*

*did raise you from infancy*

*Be humble to your mother in order to endorse you*

*For disobedience to her is one of major sins*

—Imam Shafi'ee

*Your mother has a great right, which you could fulfill easily.*

## Mother's Mercy

There is nobody in the entire earth who is more forgiven to her son than a mother. . .the child offends his mother. However, the mother's heart is always forgiving to this offence . . . . And there is no mother, no matter how bad is her habit that would not forgive her son's disobedience and rebellion. That is why Allah used a mother and her son as an example of forgiveness in order for us to know that the mercy of Allah is unlimited.

—Shiekh M. Mutawwali Sha'rawii,: "Miracle of the Qur'an."

*"I know that she was the kindest, most generous spirit I have ever known, and what is best in me I owe it to her."*

— President Barack Obama, in reference to his mother

# Chapter Four

## Instances Of Parental Disobedience and Abuse and Its Demerits

*"She was the archetypal selfless mother; living only for her children, sheltering them from the consequences of their actions and in the end doing her irreparable harm."*

—Marcia Muller

To paraphrase from the famous Islamic prolific writer and scholar, Hafiz Ibn Hajaril Asqalanii, أميرالمؤمنين في الحديث (Commander of the Faithful in Hadith compilation during his time), disobedience to parents is for a child or a man to do anything that will cause physical or psychological pain to them. This pain is usually in the form of word or action that is contrary to their wish or authority regarding matters which are not diametrically opposed to Islamic code of ethics. In the words of Hafiz Ibn Hajar al-Asqalani, the eminent Islamic scholar: "Disobedience to parents occurs when a child inflicts physical or emotional pain upon them through words or actions, contrary to their wishes, so long as these do not conflict with Islamic principles." Neglect is also a form of disobedience because it is contrary to how they related to their child when he or she was an infant under their tutelage. Parental neglect and abuse are not merely acts of disrespect—they represent a profound betrayal of the care and love parents provide from a child's infancy.

History is replete with instances of abuse, disobedience and disrespect to parents, as mentioned previously of the cases in Britain and the United States. In the United States in particular, it is very disheartening to see Muslim children blindly copying the non-Muslim ones by calling the police on their parents whenever their parents try to correct them. If these calls were to continue, they would be separated from their parents and be sent to child foster homes, which non-Muslim environment and a fertile ground for a child to be brainwashed.

### Modern Cases of Parental Disobedience

A Muslim teenager told her peers to "jump" (beat) her mother

An African woman who got divorced from her husband and was living with her four children as a single parent in the Bronx. She had a bitter experience with her fourteen-year-old daughter. An experience she will never forget for the rest of her life. She endured unimaginable abuse from her fourteen-year-old daughter.

The girl who is the oldest among her children joined a gang of peers who attend the same school and have become so notorious in their neighborhood because of their bad drinking and smoking behavior. They even smoke in front of the mother with the rest of the children looking at them. This girl stays outside for long hours after school ends and comes home very late at night.

So, one day, her mother who is about 40 years of age decided to go to her school to escort her home. When she got there, she told her daughter that she came to take her home.

The daughter refused and when the mother insisted on going home with her, she without any hesitation told her colleagues to "jump" or beat her up.

These teenagers who were five in number did as they were ordered, pouncing on the mother and beating her mercilessly. They nearly killed her, had it not been for the intervention made by a Good Samaritan who called 911, she would not have survived. This mother, who had already faced the challenges of divorce and raising her children alone, was left traumatized.

It will interest you to know that this girl still lords it over her mother in their apartment. She told her mother with an aura of authority that, whenever she is sitting in the living room she should stay in the bedroom and vice versa. She added that this order should be abided especially whenever her friends come into the apartment. The daughter's justification? The apartment, provided by city authorities, was "theirs," not her mother's. Her audacity even extended to restricting her mother's movements within their home.

She said this, reasoning that her father does not stay with them anymore and the city housing authority left the apartment for her and her young brothers and not for her mother.

In fact, since this unfortunate incident, the mother has never been to her school again, because the daughter warned her not to do so, or else her deviant colleagues would kill her.

This is a clear case of a girl going out of control and the other similar incidents listed below support the statement made by the Prophet (S.A.W)in a long Hadith narrated by

Umar in which the angel appeared to the Prophet (S.A.W) and started asking him series of questions, including events that indicate that mankind is approaching the end of time and one of the sign she revealed is:....أن تلد أل مةبوتةها ...", "A servant of (Allah) or mother would give birth to her goddess or deity...."

According to some scholars the Hadith implies that there will come a time when children will be in full control of their parents, which is contrary to the norm in any society. This tragic case exemplifies the prophecy of the Prophet Muhammad (S.A.W), highlighting a time when children will dominate and control their parents—a reversal of the natural order.

## Sons Threaten Their Father with Guns

There was an instance when a Muslim father was put under "house arrest" by his two children whom he brought from Ghana not long ago. Realizing how notorious they turned out to be, he advised them several times and did not see any change in their bad behavior. He began to put some 'fear' into them by telling them that if they do not turn a new leaf of life, he would send them back to Ghana. Frustrated by their unruly behavior, he threatened to send them back to Ghana. Because they felt uncomfortable whenever he said this, the young adults decided to teach him a lesson. They secured two guns and approached their father while he was sitting in their family apartment. One of them stood in front of him with the gun and the other stood behind him. Both of them started hitting him with the gun and saying, "You better stop saying you will take us to Ghana, if you do not want to be killed with these guns."

This is a clear case of children out of control and not too long after this incident, these kids were arrested when the police found drugs and guns on them and they are now languishing in jail.

This is a clear testimony of the Hadith of the Prophet (S.A.W) that says, "Disobedience to parents is a sin that brings punishment in this life before the Hereafter." And also "Allah keeps all acts of violation or sin on this earth till the Day of Judgment with the exception of disrespect and disobedience to parents, for the culprit will see the negative repercussion and ramification in his life on earth before meeting the worst punishment of hellfire in the hereafter if he does not repent."

## Heartbreaking Tales of Betrayal

### A Doctor Degrades His Farther to Impress a Woman

There was this man whose father took care of him and educated him up to the doctorate level that man displayed gross ingratitude. Upon becoming a doctor, he wanted to get married to a very beautiful girl that was being sought after by dozens of men. To win her favor, he therefore lied to her that he was from a very rich family and his father owns a huge fleet of cars and numerous edifices. One day, she requested to visit his 'rich' family. They went to a village and upon their arrival, his father, dressed in tattered clothes, came back from the farm. This man had the audacity to tell this lady that "this man is one of my father's workers." His father could not believe his ears and said in amazement: "What did you say, my son?" It was then that this girl realized that this doctor lied to her; she became furious and gave him a heavy slap on the face for depicting his father in such a demeaning and degrading way. She decided not to marry him because of this attitude towards his father in a bid to win her heart. The father's heartbreak serves as a cautionary tale about the consequences of abandoning family values for personal gain.

## A Man Stabbed His Mother to Death for Her Disapproval of His Choice of Wife

This was a mother who wanted her son to marry a girl with a much higher sense of morality and piety than the girl he preferred to marry. As she tried to convince him  about the consequences of his action, he argued with her to the point where he took a knife from the kitchen and stabbed her, killing her instantly just because of a girl she does not want him to marry. This act of unspeakable cruelty haunted him for the rest of his life, as he realized the weight of his crime.

Many are those mothers who wished they never delivered those children because of these acts of inhumane and wicked treatment by them. Witnessing such acts, they lament their sacrifices, questioning how children they nurtured with love could commit such atrocities.

## A Man Moved His Mother Out of His House Upon The Request Of His Wife

Once there was this man living with his mother. Later on when he got married, his wife moved in with them. This wife had the courage to tell him to move his mother out of the house. She said they cannot have peace of mind unless this old woman is taken away from them. When he was reluctant to move her away, this woman told him to choose between her and his mother. Succumbing to his wife's demands, this man unbelievably carried his aged mother on his back and took her to a valley at night. He threw her into the valley and left her there. Later upon sober reflection, he disguised himself in order not to be recognized and passed by her. He saw her crying and he asked her, "why are you crying dear old lady?" She said, "my son left me here and I entertain fears that a lion might attack and kill him on his way home. "He then asked, "Are you crying and feeling for him and not cursing him in spite of this bizarre and evil act of his?"

She answered him with the natural tender-heartedness befitting a mother by saying, "my heart bleeds whenever I think of any harm against him."

Regretting his bad deed, he returned her to his house. Having noticed his wife's enmity towards his mother, he divorced her and sent her out of his house.

## The Long-Lasting Impact of Disobedience

## He Favored His Wife Against His Mother And Could Not Proclaim The *Shahada*

In a long Hadith related on the authority of Abu Hurairah, may Allah be pleased with him said: "During the era of the Prophet (S.A.W), there was a man called Alqamah who was very pious. He was fond of *kiyamul lail* (night supplication) and fasting and many acts of kindness recommended by the Quran and Sunnah. He suddenly became sick and was on the verge of death and the people surrounding him were trying to recite the *kalimatu shahada* (final words of declaration), which once declared by a dying person fortified his faith in Allah which is *Laa'ilaaha illalLah*; (There is no deity worthy of worship except Allah) to enable him recite after them before his death. After several attempts were made to enable him to say the simple and easy words, he could not utter it. They then sent one of them to inform the Prophet (S.A.W). The Prophet (S.A.W) upon arrival predicted that there might be a problem between him and his mother. He then sent a *Sahabah* to call his mother. When she came, the Prophet asked her, 'what was the relationship between you and your son?' she said:

'He always favors his wife whenever she disrespects me.' The Prophet (S.A.W) concluded that 'it was because of this attitude towards you that Allah held his tongue and is unable to utter the *kalimatu shahada*, so please forgive him."

She appeared reluctant to forgive him, so the Prophet (S.A.W) ordered the *sahabah* to gather pieces of firewood and burn him alive. However, upon this move, out of motherly empathy, she forgave him and in a twinkle of an eye, he recited the *shahada* and passed away."

## One Bad Turn Deserves Another

Ponder over the case of this old man who was crying while his son was slapping and smacking him on the face by the pavement. And

when some passers-by approached the boy in an attempt to stop him, the father himself told them to leave him alone saying, "in fact, I slapped and smacked my father 20 years ago on the same spot and now I realized that parental abuse is a loan or debt that one is bound to pay back in the future."

## What Is Good For The Goose Is Good For The Gander

A young kid also saw his father trying to drag his old grandmother away from his house and when this boy asked why he is trying to move her away from the house, the father said, "I am fed up with her. This boy with so much tender heartedness toward his grandmother cried bitterly and said to his father, "we will do the same thing to you one day if you do not return her to us." Having reflected on the effect of the boy's vow, he regretted his action and took her back to the house.

## He Asked His Father for Money, Then Killed His Father

A story was told of a boy who was living a deviant life of gambling, drunkenness and fornication. He requested some money from his father to go and spend in his wayward life. When his father refused to give him the money and told him that he will rather spend the money on his young ones' school and stationery needs as well as their feedings, he became furious and left the house. He however came back later in the night with a heavy metal and hit his father with it who was deep asleep and the father died instantly.

## The Consequences Of Rejecting A Mother's Choice Of A Wife

There was a case of a man whose mother gave him a wife to marry. After marrying her, he realized she had no secular education and he divorced her. However, after he married a new woman with secular education, she stopped eating his mother's food, disrespected her and even told him to move his mother out of the house. He did as she requested and within few months, he became poor, lost his job and she divorced him. This man experienced a multi-dimensional crisis as a result of violation of his mother's advice by divorcing her choice of a wife and also moving her out at the expense of his rude and disrespectful wife.

## He Came Back from Europe to 'Pay' His Mother For Breastfeeding Him

Above all, the most bizarre and incredible among these stories is an incident that happened in one of the African countries. The source of this story was from a young Muslim teacher now living in New York, who happened to be with the scholar involved in the story. There was a man who went to see a scholar. When the man was asked of his mission, he told the teacher that when he lives in Germany and his mother keeps on harassing him for money, so he decided to 'pay her' for her effort in breast-feeding him by ending any family relationship between the two of them in order to have his 'peace of mind'. After these words, he dropped an amount of two thousand dollars in front of the teacher and asked the teacher to go together with him to his mother to serve as a witness as he submits his 'back payment' or a 'reciprocal reward' of her effort in raising him. The teacher could not believe his ears and eyes, as if he was watching a movie. However, upon sober reflection and having noticed the seriousness of the man, he began to advise him to ponder deeply over the pain and discomfort she had to bear just to see him become a responsible and well cultured personality that she could be proud of.

The teacher recited verses from the Holy Qu'ran that encourage obedience and kindness to parents as well as the *AHadith* to buttress his point. But it was as if it fell on deaf ears. The man left the money with the teacher, promising that he would be right back. He drove away in his red car and never came back. The teacher waited with the money months upon months and never saw him again. The teacher then decided to put the money in the coffers of the mosque as *FiisabililLah* and all this happened without the mother's knowledge. This man left the country conscious of the fact that the money was meant to 'reimburse' his mother and he did not care whether it reached her or not. He ex-communicated her totally. Sooner or later, he will reap what he sowed. This story exemplifies instances of abuse, disrespect, disregard and disobedience towards parents and this is only a tip of an iceberg as compared to thousands of cases of this nature that were not yet revealed.

## Cultural and Religious Teachings on Parental Obedience

### Islamic Perspective

Islam places immense emphasis on the rights of parents, particularly mothers. Sheikh Muhammad Mutawalli Sha'rawi eloquently explained: "A father's sacrifices are visible to a child—he provides for their needs. But a mother's sacrifices are hidden, as she carries the child through the unseen pains of pregnancy, childbirth, and nurturing. Hence, Allah commands greater obedience to mothers, for their contributions are often unrecognized."

The Prophet Muhammad (S.A.W) repeatedly emphasized the mother's precedence: "Your mother, your mother, your mother—then your father." (Sahih Bukhari)

## Obedience To Mothers Is A Top Priority

Allah the Al-Mighty, in His recommendation towards mothers has chosen her first because she plays an invisible role in the life of her child or a role which is beyond the child's comprehension.

This is because a mother is responsible for the entire process of his development right from the womb to his delivery and his baby sitting . . . until he becomes an adult. When he grows up and begins to mature, he finds his mother at the forefront of fulfilling his needs.

Hence the virtues or merits of father is obvious in the sight of the child....But the virtues or roles of the mother is hidden ...So that is why the order (from Allah) towards motherly obedience and kindness appears more than the father, because the child would always realize and appreciate the role his father plays whiles he is providing his needs, but he could hardly tell and value the sort of effort his mother went through.

—Sheihk Muhammad Mutawalii Sha'arawii

*"There will never be a pillow in the earth more comfortable than the lap of a mother."*

—William Shakespeare

*"I am indebted with all that she provided to me and I vow to dedicate all that I achieve to my mother exclusively."*

—Abraham Lincoln

*"I know that she was the kindest, most generous spirit I have ever known, and what is best in me I owe it to her."*

— President Barack Obama, in reference to his mother

## Conclusion

The stories in this chapter serve as both warnings and lessons. Parental disobedience is not just a violation of societal norms but a spiritual crime with dire consequences in both this world and the Hereafter. Honoring parents, particularly mothers, is a cornerstone of faith and morality.

Let these narratives remind us to cherish and respect our parents, recognizing their sacrifices as the foundation of our success and well-being.

*"I will never feel comfortable unless I am on the laps of my mother."*

—Socrates, Philosopher

# Chapter Five

## Qur'anic Injunctions On Obedience Towards Parents

*"There never was a woman like her; she was gentle as a dove and brave as a lioness . . . . The memory of my mother and her teachings were, after all, the only capital I have made my way."*

—Andrew Jackson

*"The Lord has decreed that you worship non but Him, and that you be kind to parents whether one or both of them attain old age in your life. Say not to them a word of contempt, nor rebel them but address them in terms of honor." "And, out of kindness, lower to them the wing of humility and say: 'My Lord! bestow on them your mercy even as they cherished (raised) me in childhood.'"*

--Q: 23-24

## Commentary & Analysis:

According to Yusif Ali's commentary on this verse (and the rest of the verses below): A critical look at the above verse reveals that the spiritual and moral duties are intertwined. We are to worship none but Allah, because none but Him alone is worthy of worship not because of "the lord your God is jealous God, visiting the iniquity of the father upon his children unto the third and fourth generation of them that hate me". Exodus -20:5.

Note that the act of worship may be collective as well as individual; hence the plural, *ta'buduu* (you worship). Kindness to parents is an individual act of piety; hence the word, *falaa-taqul*(to say).

In the second verse, the metaphor used is that of a high-flying bird which lowers her wing out of tenderness to her offspring. There is a double meaning:

First, when the parent was strong and the child was helpless, parental affection was showered on the child. So when the child grows up and is strong and the parent is helpless, can he do less than bestow similar tender or care on the parent? It is a big question for you to ponder upon!

Second, he must approach the matter with gentle humility. For does parental love not remind him of the love with which Allah cherishes His creatures? There is something here more than simple human gratitude: It goes up into the highest spiritual order.

"We have enjoined on man kindness on his parents: In pain did his mother bear him, and in pain did she give his birth. The carrying of the child to his weaning is (a period of thirty months). When he reaches the age of full years, he says:'Oh, my Lord! Grant me that I may be Grateful for Your favor which You have bestowed upon me and upon both my parents and that I may work righteous such as You may approve. And be gracious to me in my issue. Truly have I turned to You and truly do I bow to You in Islam.' Such are they from whom we shall accept the best of their deeds and pass by the ill deeds (they shall be) among the Companions of the Garden: a promised truth, which was made to them (in this life). But (there is one) who says to his parents, 'Fie on you! Do You hold out the promise to me that I shall be raised up, even though generations have passed? (rising again)' And (re-but the Son): 'Woe to you have faith! For the promise of Allah is true.' But they say, 'This is nothing but tales of the ancients.'"

—Q: 15-17.

## Commentary & Analysis:

The time of weaning was stated to be the age of two years, twenty-four months. Six months is the minimum period of human gestation (when he becomes a toddler)after which the child is known to be viable. This is in accordance with the latest ascertained scientific facts that the average period of weaning is much less than twenty-four months.

The maximum period of breast feeding (two years) is again in accordance with the time that the first dental tooth is ordinarily completed in a human child. The lower milk incisors (the first set of teeth that grows in the mouth of infants) in the center come out between the sixth and ninth months; the milk teeth grow in intervals until the canines(relatively long pointed teeth)appear. The second molars (the foremost and most complicated teeth) come out at the twenty-four months and with them the child has a complete apparatus of milk teeth. Nature (Allah) now expects him to chew and masticate and be independent of his mother's milk completely. On the other hand, it hurts the mother to feed from the breast after the child has a complete set of milk teeth. The permanent teeth begin at the sixth year and the second molar comes at the twelfth year.

The third molars are the wisdom teeth, which may appear at eighteen to twenty years or not at all.

The age of full strength (*a-shudd*) is held to be between eighteen and thirty or thirty-two. Between thirty and forty, the man is in the peak of manhood. After that, he begins to notice his aging and rightly commends the new generation to Allah. Usually, his spiritual faculties also gain the upper hand after forty.

The child who matures over the years from child to adult may prove himself to be an ungodly son who flouts all that the pious father or mother held sacred and who looks upon them as old-fashioned and unworthy of respect or regard. The contrasts found in an individual family may be matched by the contrasts in the passing and rising generations of mankind. All this happens as a passing phase in the normal evolution of mankind. And there is nothing in this to be despondent about. What we must do is ensure that the mature generations bring up their successors in godly ways and for younger ones to realize that age and experience count for something, especially in the understanding of the spiritual matters and other issues of human concern. Verses-14-15:

*"And we have enjoined on man (to be good) to his parents: In travail (painful labor) upon travail did his mother bear him and in two years was his weaning:(hear the command)."Show gratitude to me and to your parents: To Me is (your final) abode. But if they strive to make you join in worship with Me things of which you have no knowledge, obey them not: Yet bear them company in this life with Justice."(and consideration) and follow the way of those who turn to Me(in love):In the end, the return*

*of you all is to Me and I will tell you the truth (and meaning of all that you did.)"*

## Commentary & Analysis:

The set of milk teeth in a human child is completed at the age of two (as mentioned in the other verse) which is therefore the natural extreme limit for breast feeding. In our artificial life the duration is much less. Where the duty to man conflicts with the duty of Allah, it means that there is something wrong with the human will and we should obey Allah rather than man. But even here it does not mean that we should be arrogant or insolent to parents and those in authority. We must be kind, considerate and courteous, even when they command things which we should not do, like worshipping of false things (idols) which are alien to our true knowledge, things that go against our own pure nature as created by Allah.

In any apparent conflict of duties, our standard should be Allah's will, as declared to us by His command. That is the way of those who love Allah. Their motive is disobedience to parents or human authority where disobedience is necessary by Allah's law. It is not self-willed rebellion or defiance, but love of Allah, which means the true love of man in the highest sense of the word.

And the reason we should give is: "Both you and I have to return to Allah: Therefore, not only must we follow Allah's will, but we must command nothing against Allah's will."

These conflicts may appear to us strange and puzzling in this life. But, in Allah's presence, we shall see their real meaning and significance. It may be that that was one way in which our true mettle could be tested: for it is not easy to disobey and love man at the same time.

These verses reiterate the duties of **respect, empathy, and gentle speech.** Even if parents urge wrongdoing or disbelief, the child remains obligated to treat them with courtesy and compassion in worldly affairs.

## He Embarked Upon Hajj For His Mother And Saw Her In A Dream

King Usamat Bun Munqaz narrated that: There was once a Muslim called Umay Nasr who went to perform Hajj on behalf of his deceased mother. He then saw her in his dream reciting this poem for him praising him for his obedience, respect and kindness to her and above all performing Hajj in her name which she could not make when she was alive.

## Man Is Still An Infant Until His Mother's Death

*Where you are my Mother . . . .*

*Where are you my Compassion . . . .*

*Where are you my Soul. . . .*

How can life be comfortable after you, and how can I feel delighted after your departure from me. I never knew that I would feel the impact of the huge vacuum since your departure for ever until my death. Verily, the distress and pain have increased . . . .How can he be comfortable to laugh and live in peace he who lost his mother.

## Mother O' Mine

*If I were hanged on the highest hill,*

*Mother O' mine' Mother, O'Mine!*

*I know whose love would follow me still,*

*Mother O'Mine, O'Mother O'mine!*

*If I were drowned in the deepest sea,*

*Mother O'mine, O'Mother, O'mine!*

*I know whose tears would come down to me,*

*Mother O'mine, O' Mother O'mine!*

*If I were damned of body and soul,*

*I know whose prayers would make me whole.*

*Mother O'mine O mother O'mine!*

—Rudyard Kipling

*"There is not a relationship in a family that is more important than
the relationship a child has with (his or) her mother."*

—Michelle Obama, First Lady of the United States

# Chapter Six

## Ahadith (Wisdom) Of The Prophet (S.A.W) On The Effect Of Parental Disobedience

*"Who is that who loves me and will love me forever with an affection which no chance, no crime of mine can do away? It is you, my mother."*

—Thomas Carlyle

## Mothers Deserve Much More Companionship Than Fathers

On the authority of Abu Hurairah, may Allah be pleased with him who said, a man came to the Prophet (S.A.W) one day and asked, "Oh Prophet (S.A.W), who is the rightful person to deserve my companionship?" The Prophet (S.A.W) said,"*ummuka* (your mother)," and he said, "then who?" The Prophet said, "*ummuka* (your mother),""and then who?" the Prophet (S.A.W) said, "*ummuka*," and when he asked the same question for the fourth time, the Prophet (S.A.W) said, "*abuuka* (you father)"only once.

From the afore mentioned Hadith, it can be easily understood that the Prophet (S.A.W) mentioned "mother" for three consecutive times before mentioning "father" only once, meaning he took the welfare of mothers with all the seriousness it deserves, by virtue of the fact that they play the most difficult role in the life of children. He was raised by three different mothers. The first was his own biological mother, Aminah, who died on her way back from a journey at *Abuwa*, a village between Makkah and Madinah when the Prophet (S.A.W) was about six years of age. He was then raised by Barakatul Habashiyyah(an Ethiopian), who was his mother's house help at the time. Before living with Barakatul-Habashiyyah, Halimatu Sa'adiyah was his wet nurse or foster mother for two years. So it was not out of place that he had an intuition from Allah to make such a powerful pronouncement regarding mothers, by virtue of the love, affection and compassion he had attracted from each one of them during infancy.

## Preferring Parental Obedience Above Worship

On the authority of Abu Hurairah, may Allah be pleased with him said, the Prophet (S.A.W) may the peace and blessings of Allah be upon him said: "No body spoke in a cradle except three babies; Issah (Jesus), Ibrahim and Juraij."

Juraij used to be highly religious and pious. He erected a tent to be in seclusion and meditation. His mother came to him one day and met him making *salat* (prayer). She called him, "Juraij" (wanting to talk to him). He said, "Oh Lord! my mother or my *salat*?" (in a dilemma as to which to attend to). He decided to continue with his *salat*. The mother then turned away and left. She however came back the next day and found him in the same mood as the previous day. She called him, "Oh Juraij." He said, "Oh Lord, my mother or my *salat*?" He continued with the *salat,* and she left. She came the next morning and met him making *salat* again and called him the third time and he repeated the same statement he made the two previous nights.

Upon ignoring her for three days in a row, she then prayed, "Oh Lord, do not take his soul until he looks at the face of a prostitute."

And Juraij happened to be in the community of Banu Israil, who started talking about him, his piety and devotion to Allah. There happened to be a beautiful prostitute or whore among them who was very promiscuous. This lady said to them: "If you want I could put him in a test for you." They agreed. She then went to his tent and stood behind him, but he did not turn to look at her. She then went to a shepherd who was busy in his tent and seduced him. Having been unable to resist her temptation, he had an intercourse with her and she became pregnant soon after. When she gave birth, she claimed that the father was Juraij. The people took him away from his tent, destroyed it and started whipping him. He asked them what is their issue with him and they said, "you have fornicated with this girl and she gave birth." They brought the baby and Juraij told them, "Let me pray and come back." He left them to make supplication and afterwards came to the baby, touched its stomach and asked, "Oh baby, who is your father?" The baby answered him saying, "the shepherd." Upon the baby's amazing reply and out of guilty consciousness, they approached Juraij, trying to kiss him and even promising to build his cell with gold and diamond, but he told them to build it as it was with clay."

This is quite a long Hadith and the first part mentioned above has a direct impact on the subject of the discussion. It indicates how Allah answered the prayer of the mother of Juraij despite Juraij's piety and supplication to Allah. Due to the power of mothers' prayers towards their children, which Allah answers in a twinkle of an eye, the Prophet (S.A.W) in another Hadith urged mothers not to pray to their children in negative manner or wish them doom.

Woe unto He who Met His Parents and Did not Enter Paradise

In another Hadith, also reported by Abu Hurairah, the Prophet (S.A.W) may peace and blessings of Allah be upon him said:

*"Woe unto him and woe unto him and woe unto him." And the sahabah sitting by him curiously asked, "who, oh Messenger of Allah, he has really failed and lost a great deal?" The Prophet (S.A.W) answered, "He who met his parents in their old age one or both of them and he did not enter paradise."*

The Hadith indicates that those who meet their parents alive should count themselves blessed for having a window of opportunity to serve them in a bid to enter *Jannah*.

Obedience to Parents Increases One in Age and Wealth:

On the authority of Anas Bun Malik, may Allah be pleased with him, the Prophet (S.A.W) may the peace and blessings of Allah be upon him said, "He who will be happy to see himself being wealthy should be obedient and kind to his parents." And in another Hadith a man asked the Prophet (S.A.W), "is there anything that remains for me to do in terms of kindness to my parents after their death?" The Prophet (S.A.W) said, kindness and prayer to them and seeking for forgiveness for them and respecting and honoring their kith and kin or close relations."

Allah Keeps All Sinful Acts and Will not Punish Mankind until the Day of Judgment, Except Parental Disobedience

On the authority of Abdullah Bin Masud, may Allah be pleased with him said, the Prophet (S.A.W) may the peace and blessings of Allah be upon him said, "Allah keeps all sinful acts and would not punish mankind until the day of judgment, with the exception of parental disobedience.

For Allah will render his punishment on the disobedient and disrespectful one, here in this world before his or her death."

So that is the main key to Jannah that every Muslim wishes to enter to enjoy its unimaginable and incredible luxury. It is therefore important for every Muslim to be closer to his parents, mothers in particular and make them your best companions.
Mothers have the absolute right to be with you, because the more they see you or hear your voice, the more you penetrate their hearts with joy and happiness. It is even said that distancing oneself from his parents loses him or her a lot of benefits or goodness.

Ahadith (Wisdom) of the Prophet (S.A.W) on the Effect of Parental Disobedience

"The pleasure of Allah lies in the pleasure of the parents, and the displeasure of Allah lies in their displeasure." (Sunan al-Tirmidhi)

Honoring parents is not merely an act of kindness in Islam—it is an obligation second only to worshiping Allah. The Prophet Muhammad (S.A.W) emphasized this responsibility repeatedly, associating it with immense rewards and dire consequences for neglect. Through authentic Ahadith and the wisdom of Islamic scholars, this chapter explores the blessings of parental obedience and the dangers of disobedience.

## Mothers Deserve Greater Companionship

A man asked the Prophet Muhammad (S.A.W): "Who among people is most deserving of my good companionship?" The Prophet replied: "Your mother." The man asked again: "Then who?" The Prophet repeated: "Your mother." The man persisted: "Then who?" The Prophet again said: "Your mother." Finally, on the fourth time, the Prophet answered: "Then your father." (Sahih Bukhari, Sahih Muslim)

### Reflection

This Hadith highlights the unique sacrifices of mothers. Their role begins from the pain of childbirth and continues through sleepless nights, constant worry, and unconditional love. The Prophet (S.A.W), having been raised by multiple maternal figures, understood this deeply. Halimah as-Sa'diyah, his wet nurse, once visited him in Madinah. The Prophet (ﷺ) (S.A.W) stood up, spread his cloak for her to sit on, and honored her as if she were his own mother.

Call to Action: Ask yourself, "When was the last time I truly honored my mother? Have I shown her the gratitude and respect she deserves?" Let this Hadith inspire you to strengthen your bond with her today.

## Parental Obedience Over Voluntary Worship

**The story of Juraij serves as a powerful lesson:**

Juraij, a devout worshipper, was in prayer when his mother called him. Torn between continuing his salah and responding to her, he chose to prioritize his prayer. This happened on three separate occasions. In frustration, his mother supplicated: "Oh Allah, do not take his soul until he has seen the face of a prostitute."

Later, a false accusation of fornication was made against Juraij, and his reputation was tarnished. After supplicating to Allah, a miraculous event occurred: the infant born of the accuser spoke, declaring his true father to be a shepherd.

### Lesson

This Hadith teaches that voluntary acts of worship should never come at the expense of parental obligations. Allah's response to the mother's dua underscores the power of a parent's prayer—whether for or against their child.

### The Opportunity of Serving Parents in Old Age

The Prophet (ﷺ) (S.A.W) said: "Woe to him, woe to him, woe to him!" When asked who he was referring to, he replied: "The one who finds his parents, one or both of them, in old age and does not enter Paradise (through serving them)." (Sahih Muslim)

### Real-Life Connection

Imagine visiting an elderly parent and seeing their face light up simply because you've made time for them. For those whose parents have passed, this Hadith serves as a poignant reminder of lost opportunities. But for those with living parents, it's a golden chance to earn Jannah.

Call to Action: Start by visiting or calling your parents regularly. Offer to help them, even in small ways. Their duas for your well-being are a priceless treasure.

## Obedience Increases Life and Sustenance

The Prophet (ﷺ) (S.A.W) said: "Whoever wishes to have his provision increased and his lifespan extended should uphold the ties of kinship." (Sahih Bukhari, Sahih Muslim)

### Reflection

By being kind and obedient to parents, you invite blessings into your life. Whether it's through wealth, health, or happiness, Allah rewards those who honor their parents.

## Immediate Punishment for Parental Disobedience

The Prophet (ﷺ) (S.A.W) warned: "Allah delays all punishments for sins until the Day of Judgment, except for disobedience to parents. For this, Allah punishes the offender in this world before their death." (Sunan al-Tirmidhi)

### Real-Life Example

A man slapped his father in public, only to face a similar fate years later when his own son treated him the same way. This cycle reflects the Prophet's (ﷺ) (S.A.W) warning: "Parental disobedience is a debt repaid in this world."

Call to Action: Reflect on your words and actions. If you've hurt your parents, seek their forgiveness immediately, for Allah's mercy follows their satisfaction.

### Kindness Beyond Death

A man once asked the Prophet (ﷺ) (S.A.W): "Is there anything I can do for my parents after their death?" The Prophet (S.A.W) replied: "Yes, pray for them, ask for their forgiveness, fulfill their pledges, and maintain ties with their relatives." (Sunan Abu Dawood)

### Inspiration

Even after parents have passed, our responsibility toward them continues. Simple acts like giving sadaqah in their name or praying for their forgiveness keep their legacy alive.

Call to Action: Take a moment to make dua for your parents today, whether they are alive or deceased. Your dua is a source of light and mercy for them.

### Jannah Beneath the Feet of Mothers

When a man asked to join Jihad, the Prophet (ﷺ) (S.A.W) asked if his mother was alive. Upon hearing that she was, the Prophet (ﷺ) (S.A.W) said: "Go back and serve her, for Paradise lies beneath her feet." (Sunan al-Nasa'i)

### Real-Life Perspective

Serving one's mother is not only an obligation but a direct pathway to Allah's pleasure. Acts of kindness, whether helping with chores, listening to her, or simply spending time with her, are all forms of worship.

Call to Action: If your mother is alive, spend time with her today. If she has passed, give charity in her name or make dua for her.

## Key Lessons

1. Parental obedience takes precedence: Voluntary worship is secondary to fulfilling parental obligations.

2. Service to parents guarantees Paradise: Serving them in their old age is a golden ticket to Jannah.

3. Immediate consequences of disobedience: Disrespecting parents brings worldly hardships.

4. Kindness extends beyond their lifetime: Prayers and acts of charity in their name are ongoing rewards.

5. Mothers hold a special status: Their sacrifices grant them a unique place in a child's life and faith.

## Conclusion: A Personal Reflection

Let the wisdom of these Ahadith inspire you to act today. Remember, parental obedience is not just about earning rewards; it's about reciprocating the love, care, and sacrifices they have poured into your life.

"My Lord, have mercy upon my parents as they nurtured me when I was small." (Surah Al-Isra, 17:24)

Your Next Step

• Visit your parents today or call them to express your love and gratitude.

• If they have passed away, make dua for their forgiveness and give charity in their name.

• Share this wisdom with others so they too can reap the blessings of serving their parents.

### Reflections from Scholars on Parental Obedience

Ibn Taymiyyah: "*The rights of parents are among the greatest obligations after the rights of Allah. Obedience to them brings blessings, while disobedience leads to worldly hardship and divine punishment.*"

Imam Ghazali: "*Kindness to parents is a continuous act of worship, for their duas are a shield against calamities, and their curses are like arrows that strike unerringly.*"

Imam Abu Hanifa: "*When my mother called me, I would never raise my voice, for her call was more important than any scholar's summons.*"

Sheikh Abdul Qadir Jilani: "*To earn the pleasure of Allah, seek the pleasure of your parents, especially your mother, for her dua carries you through the storms of life.*"

Some scholars have the opinion that whenever a child or an adult leaves his parents, he inflicts some inherent psychological pain in their hearts because they tend to lose hope of seeing this child once again before their death. A man who came from Yemen approached the Prophet (S.A.W) and said he wanted to participate in *Jihad* (Holy War). The Prophet (S.A.W) asked him, "is your mother alive? "He said, "yes". And the Prophet (S.A.W) said, "go back and devote your service to her. Your Jannah is beneath her feet."

Remember that fulfilling their needs should be of the utmost priority, just like the needs of your wives and children. The Hadith says the results of obedience or otherwise will be manifested, even on this earth before the eternal life. Meaning this will reflect in the day-to-day affairs of any person who disobeys or obeys and expresses kindness to them.

A woman came to the Prophet (S.A.W) and asked him, "My mother refused to embrace Islam and I want to distance myself from her. What is your opinion?" the Prophet (S.A.W) advised her not to distance herself from the mother but obey and respect her in spite of her refusal to accept Islam.

The Prophet (S.A.W) used to go to his mother's grave to cry and seek for forgiveness for her. He used to show a great deal of respect to one of his mothers, Halimatu Sa'adiyah, who was his wet nurse and whenever he saw her in Madinah he would rise up as a symbol of respect and pray for her. He would even spread his scarf for her to sit on.

When his favorite wife, Aisha asked him who that person was, he would say," هي أميبـعد أمي "(she was my mother after the death of my (blood) mother).

A man came to the Prophet (S.A.W) and said he had committed a very serious sin and wanted to know if there is any chance of repentance. The Prophet (S.A.W) asked him, "is your mother alive?" He said, "no." The Prophet (S.A.W)asked further, "do you have an aunt?" He said, "yes." The Prophet (S.A.W) then advised him to express his obedience and kindness to her. This Hadith implies that because of blood relation to your mother, similar kindness could be rendered to her sisters when she dies and this is a means of answering one's prayer. This is an authentic Hadith related by Imam Tirmidhii in his *sunan*. The famous luminary and galaxy of Quranic Interpretation Abdullahi Ibn Abbass said, "two things are not separate from each other: Obedience to Allah and his

Messenger, *Salat* and *Zakat* and expressing your thanks to Allah and your parents."

There was a man who approached Ibn Abbass and said, "I have proposed to a woman and she refused to marry me. However, a different person proposed to her and she agreed to marry him and I killed her out of jealousy. Will my repentance be accepted?" Ibn Abbass asked him, "is your mother alive?" He said, "no." He then told him, "seek for Allah's forgiveness and devote yourself in prayer to him according to your ability." When he left, the narrator of this Hadith said, "I then asked Ibn Abbass why he asked him about his mother and he said, "I do not know any work closest to Allah than obedience to mothers."

Aisha the mother of the faithfuls may Allah be pleased with her also narrated that a woman who was fond of soothsaying, charm, magic and associating partners with Allah arrived in Madinah, wanting to know if she could repent. Aisha said, "I saw her crying when she realized the Prophet (S.A.W) was not alive to solve her problem. She even lamented that, 'my repentance will not be accepted.' I (Aisha) then asked the *sahabah* of the Prophet (S.A.W), 'this woman came to ask about repentance, but the Prophet (S.A.W) is dead. She was so sad that she did not meet him and she is here to ask you, the *sahabah*.' Then the woman said, 'I used to work magic, worship idols and do other acts of *shirk* or polytheism. How do I repent?' None of the *sahabah* knew what to say, because nobody wanted to advise her upon what he did not know. They only told her that, 'had your parents or either one of them been alive it would have sufficed you a means of repentance by expressing kindness to them." This was related by Imam Hafiz Ismael Ibin Kathir in his great Encyclopedia of History (" البلاية والنهاية")"The Beginning and the End".

## The Right of A Child

There is the need to determine the right of the child regarding breast-feeding for approximately two years. And when the child matures from the lactation stage to the stage of kindergarten, a competent person should take care of him or her. And this should be decided by the mother. Because a baby in its infancy does not need to have good mental capacity. But it needs compassion and tender-heartedness in conformity with the instinct of a mother.

It is not an orphan the one whose parents have passed away and left him, to face the harsh and difficult life circumstances . . . . But an orphan is the one who finds his mother alive but detached from him or a father who is always busy.

A child always grows on the manners his father is used to.

If you straighten a branch of a tree (prematurely), it would stand straight. But you cannot soften a timber when it is matured.

## To My Mother

*Because I feel that, in the Heavens above*

*The angels, whispering to one another,*

*None of devotional as that of "Mother"*

*Can find, among their burning terms of love,*

*Therefore by that dear name I long have called you.*

*You who are more than mother unto me,*

*And fill my heart of hearts, where Death installed you*

*In setting my life free.*

*My mother-my own mother, who died early,*

*Was but the mother to the one I loved so dearly.*

*And thus are dearer than the mother I know.*

*By that infinity with which my wife*

*Was dearer to my soul than soul-life.*

— T.S.Bell

*"The most important thing a father can do for his children is to love their mother. "*

--- Theodore Hesburgh

# Chapter Seven

The Commandments from the Holy Torah About the Significance of Honouring Mothers

*"There will never be a pillow in this world more comfortable and convenient than the lap of mothers."*

—Vernon Jordan

## Ponder Over These Wonders of Mothers

Just like the two previous chapters heighted (Qur'ah & Bible), the Torah has also plethora of stanzas urging children to be caring and compassionate toward their mothers.

Here are twelve beautiful verses to honor your mother or grandmother:

Here are twelve beautiful verses to honor your mother or grandmother:

### Honor Father and Mother (English & Hebrew)

### Exodus 20:12

Honor your father and your mother, so that your days may be long upon the land which Adonai your God has given you.

### Leviticus 19:1-3

And Adonai spoke unto Moses, saying: Speak to all the congregation of the children of Israel, and say to them: You shall be holy, for Adonai your God is holy. Everyone of you shall be in awe [or: fear] of his mother and father, and keep my Sabbaths: I am Adonai your God.

### Rashi on Leviticus 19:3:2

EVERYBODY OF YOU SHALL FEAR HIS MOTHER AND HIS FATHER: Scripture mentions the father before the mother because it is manifest to God that the child honors the mother more than the father, because she endeavors to win him over by kindly words. Therefore, by mentioning the father first, Scripture emphasizes the duty of honoring him (Kiddushin 30b).

### Rabbi Joseph Telushkin

### From Jewish Literacy, p.580:

There are two general injunctions in the Torah regulating how one is expected to feel and act toward one's parents: The fifth commandment [found in in Exodus 20:12] commands that one honor them, while [the verse in Leviticus 19:3] states: "Let each man be in awe of his mother and father, and keep my Sabbaths." What is strangely lacking in the Torah is a commandment to love one's parents, even though the Torah has no compunctions about commanding love in other relationships; people are told to ["Love your neighbor as yourself" (Lev. 19:18); "And you shall love the Lord your God" (Deut. 6:5); "You shall love the stranger" (Lev. 19:34)].

Perhaps it was believed that in a relationship as intimate as that between parents and children, love could not be commanded; either it is present or it isn't. What can be commanded, however, are honor and awe, acts and emotions that can be expressed and acted upon even during those painful periods when love might be lacking.

According to the rabbis, "awe" means deep, abiding respect, for example as in not sitting in one's father's place at the table, or in not siding with a parent's adversary during a dispute.... Honor in Jewish law is interpreted as undertaking basic obligations towards parents, including, if necessary, supplying them with food and clothing. Because of the enormous increase in recent decades in human longevity, a far larger percentage of people live now to their eighties and even nineties than in the past; often, however, with terrible mental and/or physical infirmities. Thus, the command to honor one's parents has in many ways become much more difficult to observe.

### From Olam Magazine, Summer 2001:

In addition, many children, much as they might love their parents most of the time, go through periods of estrangement from them. Thus, what the Torah is offering us is a guideline for behavior even during those periods when we might not be feeling loving toward our parents. Even at those times when we feel our parents have not been fair to us, or even when we have seen them do something we regard as wrong, we are still obligated to honor them. (However, in instances of parents who have physically or sexually abused their children, I believe that children do not owe the parents respect or anything else for that matter.)

### Kiddushin 31a:13

When Rav Dimi came from Eretz Yisrael to Babylonia, he said: Once Dama ben Netina was wearing a fine cloak [sirkon] of gold, and was sitting among the nobles of Rome. And his mother came to him and tore his garment from him and smacked him on the head and spat in his face, and yet he did not embarrass her.

### Kiddushin 31b:14

Our Rabbis taught: What is reverence [or: awe, or: fear] and what is honor? Reverence means that the child must neither stand nor sit in the parent's place, may not contradict a parent's words, nor do anything that harms a parent's interests. Honor means that a child must give a parent food, drink, and clothing, and provide transport.

Come and hear: They asked Rabbi Eliezer how far one must go in honoring their father and mother. Rabbi Eliezer said to them: Even if a parent takes a wallet and throws it into the sea in front of his child, then the child does not embarrass them.

### Mishneh Torah, Rebels 6:10

One whose father or mother has had their "mind torn away" must care for them and behave according to the parent's mental condition until God has mercy upon them. If it is impossible for the child to stand before the parent because they cannot be compassionate, they should go and charge others with appropriate care for them [the parent].

### Rabbi Israel ben Joseph Al-Nakawa (14th c. Spain)

A son must not dishonor his father (esp. mother) in his speech. For example, when the father (or mother) is old and wants to eat early in the morning, as old men do, and the son says, "Ha! The sun is not yet up, and already you're eating!?" Or when the father (or mother) asks: "Son, how much did you pay for this coat?" and the son says, "Don't worry about it. I bought it, and I have paid for it, so it is no business of yours!" Or when a son thinks to himself: "When will this old man die so that I can be free of what he costs me?"

### Sefer HaChinukh 33:1

(1) The mitzvah to honor parents-- to honor father and mother, as the Torah says (Ex 20:12) "Honor your father and your mother." And the commentary (Kiddushin 31:2) explains, "What does it mean to 'honor'? To feed, give drink, dress, bring in, and take out."

### Sefer HaChinukh 33:2

(2) The root of the mitzvah to honor parents is that it is fitting for a person to acknowledge and return kindness to people who were good to him, and not to be an ungrateful scoundrel, because that is a bad and repulsive attribute before God and people. And to take to heart that your father and mother are the reason you exist in the world, and for that it is truly fitting to honor them in every way and give every benefit you can, because they brought you to the world, and worked hard for you when you were little. Once you take this idea to heart, you will move up from it to recognize the good of the Blessed God who is the cause of you and all your ancestors until the first man, and took you out into the world's air, and fulfilled your needs every day, and made your body strong and able to stand, and gave you a mind that knows and learns, for without the mind that God granted you, you would be "like a

horse or a mule who does not understand" (Ps 32:9). And you should think long and hard about how fitting it is to be careful in your worship of the Blessed One.

### Sefer HaChinukh 33:3

(3) Regarding the specific rules of this mitzvah, such as: Whose property should be spent on this honor, the child's or the parent's? The ruling is that it is out of the parent's if the parent has property, but if not, the child must even beg door to door in order to feed their parent...

### Sefer HaChinukh 33:4

(4) This mitzvah applies in all places and times, for males and for females any time they are able.... And one who violates it disobeyed a positive commandment, and their punishment is very great, for they are like one who ignores their Heavenly Father, and if the court is able, they force him, as we wrote above, that the court forces obedience to positive commandments.

The primary Torah verse highlighting kindness and obedience to mothers is found in Exodus 20:12 (part of the Ten Commandments), which states: "Honor your father and your mother, that your days may be long in the land that the Lord your God is giving you.". This commandment emphasizes respect and reverence towards both parents, including mothers.

**Other relevant verses from the Torah include:**

Leviticus 19:3: "Every one of you shall revere his mother and his father, and you shall keep my Sabbaths: I am the Lord your God."

**Key points to remember:**

"Honor" in this context encompasses not just outward respect, but also active kindness, obedience, and care towards one's parents.

The Torah places a strong emphasis on the importance of the mother-child relationship, highlighting the need for children to treat their mothers with kindness and respect

### Yeshiva

### The torah world Gateway

Scripture says that children are to honour and obey their parents. What I want to know is when the Torah speaks of children, what age is considered a child and when is a child considered an adult? Is a child still classified a child after his/her BarBat mitzvah? If so, when does this change? According to scripture is a working, independent person of 19 still to obey all their parents say?

The laws of honoring one's parents, as commanded in the Ten Commandments, are discussed at length in the Talmud and Codes of Law (See Shulchan Aruch, Yoreh Deah, 240). Like any part of Jewish law, they are applied with great detail, and every situation has its own application. In general, though, I feel there are two major rules of honoring one's parents that are at the root of your question (perhaps "the good news, and the bad news" depending on how you see things).

Firstly (you might see this as the "bad" news) - there is absolutely no age limit to this command. The opposite is true - once a child reaches Bar or Bat Mitzvah age, they become more obligated, as they are now responsible to fulfill all the commands. Also, as one's parents age and need more and more help to live honored lives, the children have a greater responsibility towards them. In fact, the Torah does not say a "child" must honor their parents, but commands all of us with the language "Thou shalt honor thy father and mother".

Secondly (here is what could be the "good" news) - we need to understand exactly what honoring parents entails. One never has to "obey all their parents say". Rather the command has two aspects. One needs to take care of the physical needs of their parents, including housing, food, and clothing. (Who has to pay for this is a different question - in general the parents must foot the bill).

So, when one's parents are bed-ridden, one must cook for them, feed them, help them get up and dressed and be able to be mobile to the extent they need. The other aspect is to treat them always with respect and dignity. This includes speaking nicely to them, not contradicting them, not sitting in their seat, and so on.

What is not included in honoring one's parents is having to do things that they wish but are not directly related to them. For example, one may marry against their wishes, come to live in Israel even if they object [- if this will leave them without the physical help, they need in their old age, a Rabbi should be

100

consulted], or choose to learn a particular profession the parents do not approve of.

The command of honoring one's parents does not nullify a person's own independent life. Though, indicated above, even when going against what the parents want, one is obligated to do so in a polite, humble and respectful way. Of course, for a clear ruling of which things fall exactly into every case, we would need to examine each situation in detail.

you will permit me - it could be that behind your question lies a real conflict betw If een a parent and child. If this is so, perhaps (if the situation warrants it) both the parents and child should seek the advice of a third party, such as the local Rabbi, who may be able to bring shalom to all. Usually in such cases, merely quoting the ruling of Jewish law does not help very much - and sometime even exasperates the situation.

*"A mother is the truest friend we have when trials, misery, and suddenness fall upon us. When adversity takes the place of prosperity, she clings to us, endeavoring by her kind precepts and counsel to dissipate the clouds of darkness."*

– Washington Irving

# Chapter Eight

The Biblical Advocacy About Showing Care and Compassion Towards Mothers

"The hand (of the mother) that rocks the cradle rules the world."

- William Ross Wallace

Just as in Islamic and Jewish Holy Scriptures, in the Christian faith God Alimgty had made several mentioning about the significance of mothers, and went the extra mile to adminish and advise children to be kind, caring, respectful and obedient to their mother. There are myriad of Bibilical verses in this respect and below are some of them:

When women become mothers, they give up their lives, sleep, showers, and their bodies. Like Jesus' selfless act of sacrifice—mothers are marked with stretch marks, tears, and scars from the stitches. These simple marks identify how they unhusk their lives to selflessly give all of themselves over to the task of getting cognitive instructions from God Almighty to raise up the next generation.

Whether the mothers in your life are grandmothers, step mothers, adopted mothers or aunties, the Holy Bible is replete with verses showcasing their sacrificial roles in raising children.

Below are Some Verses from the Holy Bible Honoring Mothers:

Proverbs 31:25: *"She is clothed with strength and dignity; she can laugh at the days to come."*

Proverbs 31:26: *"She opens her mouth with wisdom, and the teaching of kindness is on her tongue."*

Proverbs 31:28–29: *"Her (mother) children rise up and call her blessed; her husband also, and he praises her: 'Many women have done excellently, but you surpass them all.'"*

Proverbs 31:31: *"Honor her (mother) for all that her hands have done, and let her works bring her praise at the city gate."*

John 16:21: *"A woman (mother) giving birth to a child has pain because her time has come; but when her baby is born she forgets the anguish because of her joy that a child is born into the world."*

Deuteronomy 6:6–7: *"And these words that I command you today shall be on your heart. You shall teach them diligently to your children, and shall talk of them when you sit in your house, and when you walk by the way, and when you lie down, and when you rise."*

Luke 2:51: *"And his mother treasured up all these things in her heart."*

Exodus 20:12: *"Honor your father and your mother, so that you may live long in the land the Lord your God is giving you."*

Proverbs 1:8-9: *"Listen, my son, to your father's instruction and do not forsake your mother's teaching. They are a garland to grace your head and a chain to adorn your neck."*

Isaiah 66:13: *"As one whom his mother comforts, so I will comfort you; you shall be comforted in Jerusalem."*

Psalm 139:13-16: "For You formed my inward parts; You wove me in my mother's womb. I will give thanks to You, for I am fearfully and wonderfully made; Wonderful are your works, And my soul knows it very well. My frame was not hidden from You, When I was made in secret, And skillfully wrought in the depths of the earth; Your eyes have seen my unformed substance; And in Your book were all written The days that were ordained for me, When as yet there was not one of them."

Psalm 56:8: "You keep track of all my sorrows. You have collected all my tears in your bottle. You have recorded each one in your book."

Every mom knows what it's like to be the captain of a sinking ship. There are dishes in the sink, her boss pushed up deadlines on a project, her kids are bickering, and supper just overflowed onto the stove. But this is the beautiful mess of motherhood. She is doing her best to thrive in chaos and bring her kids on that journey too. Here are some great scriptures to offer hope!

Philippians 1:3: "I thank my God every time I remember you (mother)."

Psalm 56:3: "When I am afraid, I put my trust in you(mother)."

Proverbs 31:28–29: "Her children rise up and call her blessed; her husband also, and he praises her: 'Many women have done excellently, but you surpass them all.'"

Proverbs 31:10-12: "Who could ever find a wife like this one (mother)—she is a woman of strength and mighty valor!

She's full of wealth and wisdom, the price paid for her was greater than many jewels. Her husband has entrusted his heart to her, for she brings him the rich spoils of victory. All throughout her life she brings him what is good, and not evil."

Isaiah 66:13: "As one whom his mother comforts, so I will comfort you."

Deuteronomy 6:6–7: "And these words that I command you today shall be on your heart. You shall teach them diligently to your children, and shall talk of them when you sit in your house, and when you walk by the way, and when you lie down, and when you rise."

Proverbs 31:25: "She is clothed with strength and dignity; she can laugh at the days to come."

Proverbs 23:22-25 "Listen to your father, who gave you life, and don't despise your mother when she is old. Get the truth and never sell it; also get wisdom, discipline, and good judgment. The father of godly children has cause for joy. What a pleasure to have children who are wise. So give your father and mother joy! May she who gave you birth be happy."

Psalm 139:13-14: "For you formed my inward parts; you knitted me together in my mother's womb. I praise you, for I am fearfully and wonderfully made. Wonderful are your works; my soul knows it very well."

1 Peter 3:4: "You (mother) should be known for the beauty that comes from within, the unfading beauty of a gentle and quiet spirit, which is so precious to God."

Proverbs 31:31: "Honor her (mother) for all that her hands have done, and let her works bring her praise at the city gate."

Proverbs 31:26: "She (mother) opens her mouth with wisdom, and the teaching of kindness is on her tongue."

John 16:21 "A woman giving birth to a child has pain because her time has come; but when her baby is born she forgets the anguish because of her joy that a child is born into the world."

Luke 2:51: "And his mother treasured up all these things in her heart."

Ezekiel 19:2: "Say: What a lioness among lionesses was your mother! She bedded down among the strong young lions and reared her cubs."

Song of Solomon 8:2: "I would lead you; I would bring you to my mother's house; she would teach me what to do...I would give you some my fresh pomegranate juice."

2 Timothy 1:5: "I'm reminded of your authentic faith, which first lived in your grandmother Lois and your mother Eunice. I'm sure that this faith is also inside you."

Luke 8:21: "He replied, 'My mother and brothers are those who listen to God's word and do it.'"

Ezekiel 19:10-11: "Your mother was like a vine in a vineyard planted beside the waters; she bore lush fruit and foliage because of the plentiful water, and she produced mighty branches, fit for rulers' scepters."

Proverbs 14:1: "The wise woman builds her house, but with her own hands the foolish one tears hers down."

Proverbs 6:20-22: "My child, obey your father's godly instruction and follow your mother's life-giving teaching. Fill your heart with their advice and let your life be shaped by what they've taught you. Their wisdom will guide you wherever you go and keep you from bringing harm to yourself. Their instruction will whisper to you at every sunrise and direct you through a brand-new day."

Joshua 24:15: "But as for me and my family, we will serve the Lord."

Exodus 20:12: "Honor your father and your mother, so that you may live long in the land the Lord your God is giving you."

Proverbs 1:8-9 "Pay close attention, my child, to your father's wise words and never forget your mother's instructions. For their insight will bring you success, adorning you with grace-filled thoughts and giving you reins to guide your decisions."

Ephesians 6:1-3: "Children, if you want to be wise, listen to your parents and do what they tell you, and the Lord will help you. For the commandment, 'Honor your father and your mother,' was the first of the Ten Commandments with a promise attached: "You will prosper and live a long, full life if you honor your parents."

Leviticus 19:3: "Each of you must respect your mother and father, and you must observe my Sabbaths. I am the Lord your God."

The Bible first tells us about Eve, the first mother on earth. Although she had her faults, she took care of her husband, her children, and dedicated her life to the Lord. From Genesis to Revelation, motherhood is spoken throughout Holy Scripture as an important and high calling. Children are considered a gift, a blessing from the lord, and a reward. This mother-child relationship is intended to bring joy and happiness (Psalm 139:5-9).

In Hebrew and Greek, the word mother means mother but with a twist. Hebrew adds, "parting, point of departure, division," and in Greek, we find "source of something." In other words, birth is the point of departure from a mother as she gives life.

The Bible goes on to teach that it is vital for moms to be women of faith who teach children to love the Lord. In Titus 2:3-4, the Bible list being a mother as a high calling. When the apostle Paul wrote to encourage Timothy as he led the church in Ephesus, he described Timothy's faith heritage this way: "For I am mindful of the sincere faith within you, which first dwelt in your grandmother Lois and your mother Eunice, and I am sure that it is in you as well"(2 Tim. 1:5) because they dedicated their time, efforts, and energy into raising up Timothy as a man of faith—together. Titus goes on to say to the older women to teach the younger women to love their husbands and children because he valued how he was raised. He also realized through his upbringing mothers and grandmothers fill a unique and crucial role in our society, and children need their mothers for their well-being.

## Characteristics of a Godly Mother

Not only does the Bible speak highly of mothers, but they are also an important part of raising up the next generation and having an impact on society. Mothers are characterized by many different ways like beauty, wealth, and accomplishments, but the most important quality is a mother who loves the Lord. This doesn't mean perfection; it means she honors the Lord as best as she can in all she does. No mother will have all of these qualities but here are a few:

No mother is ever prepared to lose a child, but sadly many do because of tragic circumstances like a car accident, illness, suicide, or in perhaps the toughest of all—in the womb. She carries a heaviness that her body failed her, and she couldn't keep her child safe. No matter the circumstances, she wants to be able to talk about what might have been and the dreams she had. A wonderful way to honor her, give her courage, and hope is a thoughtful verse on how God sees her, knows her, and he's holding that child close for her.

Honoring the mothers in your life can bring a mix of emotions, and that's okay. Considering all the verses from the Holy Scriptures listed above, one or two of them are bound to make an impact on your heart. Consider adding these to a card or even engraved on a piece of jewelry. Mothers have an overwhelming task of raising up the next generation and they love their children more than life itself. It's important to honor, praise, and affirm her. As mothers, we sometimes lose sight of how we are cherished in the midst of chores, toddler tantrums, sassy teens, and the day-to-day busyness. Make sure you give her life-giving words to remind her how much she is loved.

Honor her (mother) for all that her hands have done."

But we should bear in mind that whether we call her Mom, Momma, Mommy, or Mother, that name is so much more than just a title. It rather captures the extraordinary and exceptional affection, unbreakable bond, unconditional love, and never-ending care between a mother figure and child. It's a relationship characterized by constant compassion, support, sympathy, empathy and memorable teachings,and selfless sacrifices—ones that we'll never forget, no matter how old we are.

That's why Mother's Day is so special. But matter of fact, Mother's Day should be every day.

The fact iswhy would someone who carry a child or children, some would even be twins, some triplets, some quadruplets and even beyond be remembered for only one day.

The incredible impact they have on our lives and all they do for us, it's important to remind mom just how much she means to you. And what better way than an entire day dedicated to her? To celebrate, you could make her a delicious breakfast-in-bed or buy her a thoughtful Mother's Day gift. But the most significant present is perhaps a heartfelt Mother's Day card full of meaningful Mother's Day messages and Mother's Day quotes—including biblical scriptures. Because at the heart of it all, mothers are nothing short of a gift from God.

Obedience and kindness to parents are core tenets of Islam, emphasized repeatedly in the Qur'an and Hadith. The tools and practices outlined in this chapter aim to help individuals express respect, care, and obedience towards their parents, ensuring blessings in both this world and the Hereafter.

1. The Power of Kind Words

The Qur'an emphasizes the use of gentle speech with parents: "Say not to them a word of contempt, nor repel them, but address them in terms of honor." (Surah Al-Isra, 17:23)

Practical Applications

• Avoid harsh or dismissive language: Even subtle expressions like sighing or showing impatience are discouraged.

• Address them with respectful titles: As Prophet Ibrahim (AS) addressed his father as "Ya Abati" ("O my father"), children should use terms like "my father" or "my mother" instead of their parents' first names.

• Choose your words wisely: Speak in ways that uplift and reassure your parents, avoiding unnecessary arguments or corrections in public settings.

Imam Muhammad Ibn Sireen, a respected scholar, exemplified this principle by remaining silent in gatherings when his mother was present, considering speaking in her presence without necessity a form of disrespect.

2. Financial Support

Supporting parents financially is a critical aspect of obedience, especially as they age. Parents sacrifice their resources for their children's well-being, and reciprocating this care is an obligation, not an option.

The Prophet Muhammad (ﷺ) (S.A.W) said:☐ "You and your wealth belong to your parents."☐ (Sunan Ibn Majah)

Practical Advice

• Allocate a portion of your income: Regularly provide financial aid to your parents, regardless of their financial independence.

• Fulfill their needs before your own luxuries: Prioritize their comfort, even at the cost of your desires.

• Teach your family about this duty: Encourage your spouse and children to share in this act of service, fostering a culture of mutual care.

3. Physical Service

Serving parents with your physical efforts is a direct and tangible way to show kindness. Relieving them of burdens, assisting in household tasks, or simply spending quality time with them are invaluable acts.

The Prophet (ﷺ) (S.A.W) said:☐ "Paradise lies beneath the feet of mothers."☐ (Sunan An-Nasa'i)

Action Steps

• Help with chores: Take responsibility for tasks that may be physically taxing for them.

• Prioritize their comfort: Offer massages, cook meals, or simply sit with them to ensure they feel valued.

• Accompany them: Escort them to appointments, shopping, or social events, demonstrating care through your presence.

4. Teaching and Reminding Them About Allah

For parents who may not have received formal Islamic education, it becomes the child's responsibility to share knowledge with humility and respect.

The Qur'an says: "Remind, for reminding benefits the believers." (Surah Adh-Dhariyat, 51:55)

Ways to Help

• Share Islamic teachings gently, avoiding condescension.

• Encourage regular prayer and Qur'an recitation.

• Help them memorize duas and engage in dhikr (remembrance of Allah).

5. Praying for Parents

Prayers for one's parents, whether alive or deceased, are acts of ongoing charity (sadaqah jariyah) that benefit both the child and the parent.

The Prophet (ﷺ) (S.A.W) said: "When a person dies, his deeds come to an end except for three: continuous charity, knowledge that benefits, or a righteous child who prays for him." (Sahih Muslim)

Key Prayers

• For their well-being: "My Lord! Bestow Your mercy on them as they cherished me in childhood." (Surah Al-Isra, 17:24)

• For their forgiveness: "O Allah, forgive my parents, have mercy upon them, and grant them Jannah."

6. Encouraging Family Harmony

A child's kindness to their parents extends to ensuring harmony within the family, particularly between their spouse and parents.

The Prophet (ﷺ) (S.A.W) said: "The best of you are those who are best to their family." (Sunan Tirmidhi)

Strategies

• Encourage your spouse to treat your parents with respect and kindness.

• Mediate disputes tactfully to maintain peace in the household.

• Celebrate family milestones and achievements together to strengthen bonds.

7. Understanding the Gravity of Parental Disobedience

Causes of Parental Disobedience

1. Ignorance or lack of knowledge about parental rights.

2. Arrogance or self-importance.

3. Lack of piety or fear of Allah.

4. Excessive attachment to material wealth.

5. Family disputes or broken homes.

6. Long periods of separation from parents.

Features of Parental Disobedience

• Physical or verbal abuse.

• Disregarding their advice or concerns.

- Neglecting their emotional or financial needs.

- Cutting ties or excommunicating them.

- Leaving home without their consent.

Etiquettes for a Good Child-Parent Relationship

1. Absolute obedience and kindness.

2. Prompt attention to their needs.

3. Relieving them of burdens or worries.

4. Teaching them about Islam with love.

5. Praying for their well-being, in life and after death.

6. Encouraging family harmony and mutual respect.

7. Reflecting on their sacrifices and empathizing with their experiences.

Inspirational Reflections on Death and Parental Honor

- Imam Ali (RA):□ "Death is a path everyone will walk; even the Prophet (☀) (S.A.W) walked it. Death's arrow does not miss its target. What misses today will strike tomorrow."

- Imam Shafi'ee:□ "Oh my soul, endure this world with patience, for true life lies ahead."

The inevitability of death should motivate us to honor and serve our parents while we still have the opportunity. As Jalal ad-Din Rumi poetically expressed:□ "Out beyond ideas of wrongdoing and rightdoing, there is a field; I will meet you there."

By adopting these tools, individuals can ensure they fulfill their responsibilities towards their parents in ways that are deeply rewarding in this life and the Hereafter. Let this be a guide to inspire us to act with love, respect, and unwavering commitment to those who raised us.

*"I am indebted with all that she provided to me and I vow to dedicate all that I achieve to my mother exclusively."*

—Abraham Lincoln

# Chapter Nine

## Factors That Bring About Good Parental Tutelage

*"What makes you a man is not the ability to have a child but the courage to raise one."*

--- Barrack Obama, 44th President of the United States

There are numerous ways and means of raising children to grow up to be courteous and caring to their parents and this chapter will deal at length with some of these factors that were advocated by the Qur'an and Sunnah.

## Instil In Them the Islamic Teachings and Morals:

The Prophet may the peace and the blessings of Allah be upon him said:"

"Train your children on three manners: love for the Prophet, love for his households and recitation of the Qur'an, for those who carry the Qur'an (readers) will be beneath the shadow of the throne of Allah on the day that there will be no shadow except the shadow of Allah with His custodians and friends." The Hadith implies that the father should always love the Prophet (s.a.w) and his household. He does that by way of implementing his Sunnah and that of his *sahabah* and his household as well as reading the Qur'an on daily basis which the Prophet (s.a.w) recommended to be recited completely for at least each week.

If one is unable to do so every three days, then at least within a month. Ibn Abbas even said that if one cannot read the entire Qur'an within one month (meaning two chapters each day), the person is considered as someone who has distanced himself far from the Qur'an.

While you are paying heed to this Hadith in your home and your kids are growing and observing this, they begin to develop an interest in it.

This is why it is crucial to introduce them to the Qur'an early. One effective approach is to start teaching them basic Arabic letters, as this will enable them to learn the Qur'an easily even before they start Kindergarten.

In another Hadith:

On the authority of Anas Bin Malik, may Allah be pleased with him said, "He who recites the Qur'an and works according to its principles, Allah will prepare a special crown for his parents on the day of judgment. And this crown will be brighter than the light of the sun on Earth—how much more for the one (child) who works by its letter and spirit". This Hadith was reported by Abu Dawud.

And remember, this could only be achieved if both parents, or at least one of them, reads the Qur'an regularly. This point is a testimony to the statement made by a prominent Arab poet, Ahmed Shawqii:

"Young ones from us grow on what (manners) his father is fond of or is used to."

Just observe what happens with your young brothers or sisters or even your own children when they are toddlers. The boy having known that his father put on the *kufi* (hat) to make *salat* would pick up the *kufi*, put it on his head and place his palms on his chest as if in *salat* mood when the father leaves the *kufi* on a table or chair.

Same applies to the little girl who picks her mother's veil and put it on, trying to imitate her mother as she sees her praying. This natural inclination to mimic parents makes childhood the ideal time to instill values and religious devotion. Therefore, it is at this stage that parents have to capitalize on this window of opportunity to inculcate in them the culture of devoting themselves towards *salat*, for the Prophet (s.a.w) said in another Hadith:

"Command your children to make *salat* at the age of seven and beat them (though mildly) at the age of ten (when they refuse)."

The Prophet (s.a.w) recommended beating at the age of ten, conscious of the fact that at this age a boy, although still young but can be able to distinguish between what is right from what is wrong.

Another narration by Anas states: "Command them to make salat if they can tell between left and right."

And science has proven that at the age of four, a child's brain is at its sharpest stage because by then all the cognitive structures that bring about sharp memory begin to form. From then on, any information or image that children perceive or see would get embedded in their brain. This is why early exposure to the Qur'an and Sunnah is highly effective.

With constant dedication and commitment by parents to teach them the Qur'an and Hadith from that infancy stage, they would develop "photographic memory," technically referred to as, "ideatic memory," a deep and penetrating capacity to recall what they learn as toddlers. An Arab poet puts this scientific fact in a poetic perspective when he says:

*"I see myself always forget what I learnt as an adult. And I do not forget what I learnt as an infant. However, knowledge is what you*

learn as an infant. But wisdom is what you learn as an adult." Another wise man buttressed this with these inspirational words of wisdom:

"(seeking) Knowledge during infancy is like writing on a rock (highly indelible) and (seeking) knowledge during adolescence is like writing on the water (highly erasable)."Going by the above analysis, one could deduce that, the Prophet may the peace and the blessings of Allah be upon him is the greatest scientist par excellence, especially when he advocated teaching them the Qur'an and Sunnah from infancy, as this ensures deep-rooted understanding and long-lasting influence on their character and faith. Because he was educated, inculcated and inspired in the "Divine University" of Allah the Al-Mighty and emerged with the highest distinction and a repertoire (a collection or list) of scientific prophecies that have been confirmed by the past and present scientists' factual reality. The depth of his knowledge extended beyond spiritual matters, touching on principles of psychology and education that modern science continues to affirm. Further studies indicate that if you show a child a picture or narrate a story to him or her and you later ask him or her to describe or narrate it, he or she would do that with minute detail. But when a child becomes an adult, relating the same story would find him trying to recap or recall what he had heard or seen before. This signifies the unparalleled ability of children to absorb information, making it crucial to instill ethical and moral values at an early age.

If children learn and assimilate the Shariah or Qu'ran and Hadith, they will eventually get acquainted with the Islamic code of ethics governing child-parent relationship and thereby put it into practice. Because if they do not apply this knowledge, they should be conscious of its repercussion. Another poet says:

"If you do not know (something) it is a danger in itself, but if you know it, then the danger gets worse". In other words, not knowing something itself causes one a great deal of risk. However, if they know but pretend they do not know or violate the "dos" and "don'ts", they should consider themselves in a worse form of danger or disaster.

## Adopt A Good Parent-Child Relationship:

It is important for parents to respect the personalities of their children right from infancy by refraining from calling them bad, demeaning and abusive names like "stupid boy," "idiot," and what have you. That can make huge impact on them as adults in the future. Some parents (especially fathers) are too stern and strict at home such that their kids do not feel comfortable when their fathers are at home. And they have a tendency of punishing these children for every iota of mistake that they commit. This is highly un-Islamic because the holy Quran Chapter 2, Verse 159 says:

"It is part of the mercy of Allah that you deal gently with them. If you were severe or hard-hearted, they would have broken away from you: so pass over (their faults), and ask for Allah's forgiveness for them; and consult them in affairs (of moment). Then when you have taken a decision, put your trust in Allah. For Allah loves those who put their trust (in him)." The Prophet also says:

*"Whenever compassion is eliminated from anything, it makes it ugly and whenever compassion is applied in anything, it makes ta beautiful."*

*In another Hadith, the Prophet says:*

*"Allah loves compassion or leniency in every situation."*

A wise man also said, "we can achieve through gentleness much more than with severity. Can't you see that water grinds away hard rocks?"

A man once came to Khalifa Umar Bun Khatab, (may Allah be pleased with him)and said, "Oh Amirul Muminin, my son relates to me in a bad manner (disrespects me) and is disobedient towards me." Umar invited his son and asked him, "why do you disobey your father?" The boy asked, "is there any act of disobedience by a child?" Umar said, "yes of course." The boy asked, "what then is our rights as children (before we become disobedient)?" Umar said, "a father has to choose a good mother for his child, choose a good name for him as well as teach him the Holy Qur'an."

The boy told Umar: "My father did not do none of the above, my mother was a slave owned by a fire worshipper, and he named me 'Jaalan' means someone who is always roaming and wandering around and he never taught me even a letter from the Qur'an. "Then Umar became irritated at the father and said, "go away (from me). You came to me complaining about your child's disobedience, but you rather disobeyed him before he disobeys you." In another Hadith, the Prophet says:

"Honor your children and give them good training for they are special gift to you."

As the wise say, respect is reciprocal. This applies to even your own children and this man clearly ignored the Hadith of the Prophet that implored parents to teach their kids the Qur'an which was also mentioned by Umar as one of the three duties of parents towards their children.

Imam Ali, the Fourth Khalifah advised that:

"Do not nurture your children as your parents nurtured you, for they were created for an era which is different from yours."

Remember the Quran says that: "Oh you who believe, protect yourself and your households from the hell fire, the source of which are people and stones." So ponder over this powerful injunction of the Qur'an as you conclude this point.

## Cover-Up Your Differences In The Presence Of Children:

It is normal for a husband and wife to be in conflict or at loggerheads with each other. This more often than not happens on trivial issues. There are many instances that happened in the life of the Prophet himself, his *sahaba* and the *tabi'een* (second generation). The Prophet occasionally had a hard time with his wives. There was a time he became peeved at them and excommunicated them completely for one month. He left their homes and went to seek refuge in the mosque. He never allowed anybody access to him. So when Umar wanted to see the Prophet, he asked his servant, Rabiah to seek the Prophet's permission to see him. When the servant was reluctant to allow him access, he screamed on top of his voice in order for the Prophet to hear him saying, "it's me Umar, I am not here to intervene on behalf of my daughter, Hafsat and if you want me to go and strike her head out with my sword, I am ever ready to do that. "At this point, the Prophet allowed him access but never agreed with his idea of striking Hafsah (this story was narrated in; The Life of Muhammad, written by Shiekh Hykal Husseine).

There was another instance that they isolated themselves from him. They all decided not to talk to him or have any close contact with him, because he could not meet their numerous financial demands. And in all these instances he never argued with them in front of his children. Hence, Muslim couples should be considerate of the fact that whenever any differences occur between them, they need to move behind closed doors, out of their children's sight and sound to resolve their differences. This is the only way to avoid the situation where the child would grow up in the future to disrespect his mother or father because of the demeaning attitude of the father against the mother or vice versa. After all, it takes two to tango. The Holy Qur'an chapter 3 verse 19 says:

And relate to them in a kind and compassionate manner, but if you hate them, (remember) perhaps you may dislike something and Allah makes a lot of good things in it."

There is this Hadith that says: "A believer does not divorce or get annoyed with a (wife) believer. If he despises a particular manner or character of hers, he would admire her in another." And always pray to Allah to grant you the patience to be able to contain or tolerate each other's behavior. Men should especially heed this advice, as another Hadith related on the authority of Abu Hurairah may Allah be pleased with him said:

*"Be polite and kind to women for they were created from a rib and the delicate part of the rib is the upper part, if you want to straighten it, you will break it and if you leave it crooked it will remain bent. So be polite and kind to women."*

Fudail Bun Iyaad, a great man of wisdom of the *tabi'een* generation also said:

*"I used to realize my sin from the character of my beast and my wife."*

This presupposes that if a person always worries himself with the behavior of his wife towards him, it will reflect in his inter-personal relationship with people at his work or in public and thereby incur their displeasure.

One of the means of avoiding or reducing some of the marital squabbles is right from the onset, a prospective husband has to consider and re-examine the woman he is going to marry by choosing a pious and religious one. Another Hadith says:

"You should carefully choose from where one of you releases his seed (a chosen wife to make sunnah with) for the (blood vein) or DNA is contagious". It means whatever behavior, character or mannerism that is deeply rooted in a woman is going to have a direct impact in the behavior of her children. In yet another Hadith, the Prophet cautioned Muslims by saying:

"Beware of polluted blood" and they (*sahabah*) asked, "what is polluted blood?" He said, "a beautiful woman from a bad root."

Because a woman's beauty in itself is a temptation, so with this beauty coming from the bad and corrupted background, the temptation and anxiety move from bad to worse.

As an African proverb says, "a crab does not deliver a bird." Ahmed Shawqii also said, "A mother is a school if you prepare her, you prepared a youth with a sound and healthy root or vein/DNA."

Before a husband finally decides to divorce his wife, he has to think about the consequences or the spillover effect of this action on the future of his children. Naturally, it takes the tenderheartedness of a mother and the responsibility of the father to guide and guard a child against deviant behavior. While the mother applies this natural emotional sympathy and love, the father on his part, applies or adopts a mild but stern attitude to put this child on his or her toes.

## Guard Them Against Peer Group Pressure:

Children keeping bad company is one of the most significance factors of disobedience towards parents, especially in the western world. The Holy Quran in Suratul-Furqaan, verses 27-29, talking about the effect of bad company states that:

"On the day that the oppressor or unjust man will bite his fingers (in regret) saying I would have followed the path of the Prophet. And woe on me for taking this as a friend for he has led me astray from the message after it came to me and verily the devil is the most forsaken and unaided one."

This means that he who refuses to heed the call of the Prophet (s.a.w) to follow the right path, but instead decides to let the devil mislead him to keep up with bad company, will live to regret it because there will be a far-reaching repercussion on him on the Day of Judgment.

A Hadith says:

"The similarity of a good company or a bad one is like a carrier of spray of (misk) and the gold smith, for the carrier of the spray you might smell good from him and smell bad from the gold smith." Yet in another Hadith: "Man is always on the path of his friend so each of you should consider who he befriends."

A poet added something similar to this Hadith when he said:

*"Do not ask about a man, ask about his friend, for each man imitates or emulates his friend. If he is a bad one, distance yourself from him immediately, but if he is a good one, befriend him you will be guided."*

Another poet says:

*"He who lives among the honorable ones will grow up with honor. And relating to the deviant or evil ones is not the way of honor."*

Finally, another personified this situation when he said:

"Birds of the same feathers flock together."

This underscores the importance of surrounding oneself with good company, as negative influences can shape a person's behavior and moral compass. Modern studies and Islamic teachings both highlight that a child's upbringing and environment determine their future character.

So, parents should render a sober reflection on the above words of wisdom and decide for their children the type of friends they want them to keep up with, in order to make them respectful, obedient and courteous towards them.

In addition to choosing the right friends, parents must also regulate their children's exposure to mass media, social media, and the internet, which play a powerful role in shaping young minds. The Prophet (ﷺ) (S.A.W) said:

"Entertain your hearts occasionally, for if they become weary, they will turn blind." (Sunan Tirmidhi).

This Hadith acknowledges the need for entertainment but also cautions against excess, particularly when it promotes values contrary to Islamic teachings.

## Regulate Their Use Of The Mass Media, Social Media & The Internet:

The mass media (social media) is the most powerful and effective tool for socio-cultural, political, educational and religious transformation of the youth in this contemporary world. The media is a double-edge sword; it kills and heals at the same time. It kills the morals of those who use it in a negative sense and heals those who utilize it positively.

It is rather unfortunate that here in the western world the media is so liberal and free to the extent that there is virtually no censorship of the contents in the various outlets, such as newspapers, magazines, television and the internet. Unfiltered access to the internet allows children to stumble upon inappropriate material, exposing them to values that may lead them away from Islamic teachings. As a matter of fact, despite the restrictions being placed on children to drive their minds off those outlets and periodicals, many of them get "windows of opportunity" to switch through any TV channel, glance through any magazine or newspaper and navigate any social media app and the internet website that they prefer without parental supervision or regulation. And most of the media contents in the western world are entertainment-oriented, with only few educative and ethical programs.

According to the October 2008 issue of the Awake periodical dubbed, *Your Child and the Internet*, at any given moment, millions of youths are online whether they are at home, at school, at a friend's house, or if they have internet access on a handheld device or cell phone almost anywhere. In the United States alone, ninety-three percent of youths between the ages of twelve and seventeen use the internet. In Canada, nearly half of all youths with cell phones can access the internet with them. And in the United Kingdom, a study revealed that, one in every five youths between the ages of nine and nineteen had internet access in their bedrooms. It further indicated that "if you are a parent, you are faced with a sobering reality: Your children are probably more comfortable in this new cyber world than you are and they even know how to keep you in the dark about their activities . . . they are like natives and the parents are tourists in this cyber world."

As a matter of fact, Islam is not against entertainment per se, because there is a Hadith narrated by Imam Tirmidhi that says:

"Entertain the heart in between the hours, for if the heart gets tired, it becomes blind."

However, the sort of entertainment Islam is referring to here is not the one being glorified or hyped in the western media, which is diametrically opposed to its norms and values.

With the advent of the modern political, cultural, and economic concept called "globalization," every innovation or idea introduced by the western world through their powerful mass media(social media) provokes a reaction in the third world to emulate it within a matter of days or weeks, and there is a maxim within the corporate world that puts it in a satirical manner:

"When America sneezes the rest of the [third] world (countries) would catch cold."

So the third world, especially African is being bombarded with morally corrupt media contents that mislead the youth to blindly imitate or emulate the urban sub-culture that has no regard or respect for parent, by virtue of the liberty and freedom they enjoy in those societies.

Many recent cases of parental abuse emanate from what the kids view in the movies regarding rudeness and insolence of other kids to their parents. One of these cases, as outlined in Chapter Four above was of two kids who used their guns to hit their father.

However, many Islamic establishments or societies are using the

Healing side of the media to effect change and inculcate sound ethical norms and values within the up-and-coming generation of the Muslim Ummah (masses).

These organizations in the western world are operating their own TV stations and are transmitting live on the internet and via satellite with both educative and entertaining programs that serve as an alternative to the youth.

Besides, there are many Islamic websites with both video and audio programs and are telecasting movies that are *Shariah* (Islamic ethics) compliant. Also, many Islamic bookshops both in-store and online are importing a lot of software's, DVDs, and CDs that are meant for the use of the young children to learn and have fun as well.

This will enable parents to "catch them young" with a high sense of Islamic consciousness and thereby prevent them from this peer group influence.

Below are some Islamic websites for the benefit of readers:

*www.islamchannel.tv/Europe&UK.

*www.sultan.org/a/english.

*www.aswatalislam.net.

*www.islamway.com.

*www.islamnet.com.

*www.islamonline.net.

*"A mother is the truest friend we have, when trials heavy and sudden fall upon us."*

--- Washington Irving

# Chapter Ten

## Useful Tools Towards Parental Obedience

*"A mother is the truest friend we have when trials, misery and suddenness fall upon us, when adversity takes the place of prosperity, when friends who rejoice with us in our sunshine, desert us, when troubles thicken us, still will cling to us, and endeavor by her kind precepts and counsels to dissipate the clouds of darkness, and cause peace to return to our hearts."*

—Washington Irving(1783-1859)

Man can express his kindness and obedience to his parents by going through the following factors. Some scholars say, "He who Allah guards to observe these factors should consider himself or herself very fortunate to have expressed some level of obedience and kindness towards his parents."

The first factor is oral and the one second is physical. The oral factor has to do with the tongue and it is part and parcel of the rights of parents for a child to guide against abusive and offensive words towards them, by being very polite, soft, and tender hearted. The Qur'an emphasizes the use of gentle speech with parents: "Say not to them a word of contempt, nor repel them, but address them in terms of honor." (Surah Al-Isra, 17:23).

Remember Allah has combined for the tongue two features: the first feature is kind words and the second one is to shy away from lose talks. Hence he who is blessed by Allah to always use kind words and shy away from hurtful words to his parents has partly fulfilled the act of kindness towards them. Allah mentioned this vividly in Suratul-Isra'I (Ascension) verse 23 to 24 that was quoted earlier.

Some among the earlier generation of scholars opined that if there was a word so small and disrespectful than *"uffin"* (a sign of expressing your exhaustion or being fed up with them), Allah would have advised against it.

They further observed that part of the words of kindness is for a man to refrain from calling his father or mother by their real names, but rather their fatherhood or motherhood names like "my father" or "my mother." Allah gave us a typical example in Suratul Maryam chapter 42, when prophet Ibrahim (Abraham) called his father and advised him against disobeying and associating partners with Allah saying, "oh my father, why do you worship what does not hear and does not see and would not benefit you?" Addressing parents with respectful titles, as Prophet Ibrahim (AS) did by saying "Ya Abati" ("O my father"), fosters deep respect and honor.

You could see that he did not call him by his name, but said, " my father." Here, other scholars also said that whenever a son calls his father "my father," it makes him feel big and high with the sort of responsibilities attached to this title.

Part of guarding one against his tongue is to try not to talk at a gathering where his father or mother is present unless in two situations: The first is if his talk is about knowledge and the second is if it is concerning an important business or issue. Because they regard talking in the midst of your parents without the above reasons as a sign of disrespect. It was revealed that Imam Muhammad Ibn Sireen, one of the *tabi'een* (second generation after the *sahabah*) scholars would keep mute and never talk if his mother attends a gathering where he happens to be until she leaves. A stranger asked the Imam why he becomes speechless when his mother or father shows up at an event and he answered that he regards talking in their presence as tantamount to disrespecting them. Respect, says the wise, is reciprocal and the Prophet says respect your parents and your children will respect you.

It is not justifiable for a man to always give excuses in order to run away from his parental responsibilities, especially in regard to financial commitments to them. You should not lose sight of the fact that they sacrifice more than you could think of. The Prophet Muhammad (ﷺ) said: "You and your wealth belong to your parents." (Sunan Ibn Majah).

They did everything for you and even though they did not have abundant resources, they were conscious of the fact as indicated by Martin Luther King Jr., in his book, *Call to Conscience*, that "life is hard, at times as hard as a crucible piece of steel. It has its bleak and bright moments like the ever-flowing water of a river. Life has the soothing warmth of its summers and piercing chills of its winter. God is able to lift you from the fatigue of despair to the buoyancy of hope and transform dark and desolate valleys into the sunlit path of the inner peace."

Another word of inspiration comes from a prolific American writer and charismatic orator Dr. W.W. Dyer, who says, "If we are not generous when it is difficult, we can't be generous when it is easy."

It is an understatement to say that Allah has blessed us, especially those living abroad with his abundant providence and prosperity to take care of the poor, especially our parents who are financially handicapped, but alas, we tend to ignore this fact. There are many Qur'anic and Sunnatic decrees that Allah and His messenger implored us to consider this fact as stated in the chapters above. Practical steps include allocating a portion of one's income to parents, fulfilling their needs before indulging in personal luxuries, and fostering a family culture of mutual care and responsibility.

However, since we ignore this reality, some inspired non-Muslims attest to that reality and there are numerous examples, but only a few will be mentioned below.

The American media mogul and generous celebrity, Oprah Winfrey went to South Africa a few years ago. When she met a mammoth group of poor children, she became so excited to help, stating that "now I know why I have been given so much. Now I know why." In other words, Oprah was attesting to the fact that God has blessed her and placed the means of livelihood of others in her care.

Dr. W.W. Dyer also made similar pronouncement in his book, *Attitude of Gratitude*, that "now I know why I have had so many financial blessings. I feel so grateful for all that has come my way that giving back seems to be the only avenue available." Similarly, Islam teaches that serving parents physically by assisting with chores, prioritizing their comfort, and accompanying them when needed is a direct act of kindness. As the Prophet (ﷺ) said: "Paradise lies beneath the feet of mothers." (Sunan An-Nasa'i).

Research has established that serotonin, naturally occurring substances in the body that makes us feel comfort and blissful is produced automatically in us as a result of kindness extended to the poor or needy, especially parents who are poor. It further indicated that this serotonin is produced chemically in the person, extending the act of kindness as well as the recipient of this kindness. It also improves the functioning of immune system. Just imagine this! Kindness extended, received or observed beneficially impacts the physical health and feelings of everyone involved in it. These feelings are even pronounced when the receiver is your mother (parents).

No wonder that Dai la Lama, the clergy of the Buddhists' religious temple in the Far East said, "if you want others to be happy, practice compassion and if you want to be happy practice compassion."

Professor R.W. Emerson also said that, "it is one of the most beautiful compensations of this life that no man can sincerely try to help another without helping himself...Serve and then you will be served."

## Causes Of Parental Disobedience

Ignorance or lack of education.

Arrogance or self-importance.

Lack of piety or fear of Allah.

Miserliness or stinginess.

Reluctance to share willed property to the beneficiaries.

Excessive attraction to luxury and materialism.

Divorce and separation of parents (broken home).

Distancing oneself far from the parents for a long time.

## Features Of Parental Disobedience

Physical and verbal abuse.

Acting contrary to their advice.

Neglecting their needs or necessity.

Ex-communicating them for long time.

Vacating home without their consent.

## Etiquettes That Ensure Good Child-Parent Relationship

1- Absolute obedience and kindness to them.
2- Attending to their needs with urgency and adequate service.
3- Relieving them off their burden or work.
4- Reminding them of Allah's existence and teaching them what they need to know in case they are unlettered.
5- Praying and seeking Allah's forgiveness for them, dead or alive.
6- Encouraging your wife to be kind to your mother to win her heart.
7- Reading stories of obedient children and their rewards.
8- Always thinking about being in their shoes, which will eventually happen in the future by the will of Allah.

The main theme of this poem is death. Death is a path that everybody will walk, since the Prophet (s.a.w) himself walked the same route. It further says death has a sword that does not miss its target; he who missed a sword today will not miss it tomorrow.

You, the one who embraced this [material] world, that does not last forever…You will sleep [at night] and wake up [in the morning] as a traveler …You leave the embrace of this world and hug the everlasting paradise? If you wish to enjoy the eternal bliss of paradise, then do not think you will be secured from the scorch of the hellfire.

*The heartbeat of a man tells him that,*

*Life is a matter of seconds and years.*

*Then do something [good] to be remembered after your death,*

*For the remembrance of a man is a matter of a second.*

*"Oh, son of Adam, you are just days that are numbered.*

*And whenever a day passes by, parts of you pass away."*

## A Field To Meet Every One

*Out beyond ideas of wrongdoing and right doing,*

*There is a field; I will meet you there,*

*When the soul lies down in that grave,*

*The world is too full to talk about.*

*Ideas, Language even the phrase "Each Other,"*

*Does not make any more sense.*

—Jalalu-Deenu-Rumi a celebrated Persian Poet of the 12th Century

# References

1- Holy Quran-Yusif Ali's Translation and Commentary.

2- *Sahih*-(Authentic) of Bukhari.

3- *Sahih*-(Authentic) of Muslim.

4- *Sunan* of Imam Tirmidhi.

5- *Musnad* of Imam Ahamad.

6- -*Mu'hjizatil Qu'ran* (Miracle of the Qur'an). By Shiekh

7- Muhammad Mutawwalii Sha'araawii.

8- Bidayah-Wal-Nihayat(the Beginning and the End) of Imam

9- Muhammad Hafiz Ismael Ibin Kathir.

10- *Tariiqal-Madinah* (the Madinan Way) of Hujjatul-Islam Imam Ibn

11- Taymiyyah.

12- *Badarul-Munir* (The Beaming Moon),an ancient Arabic Litrature,

13- By Jibran Ni'amata Lah.

14- *Qisasul-Tabi'iiyaat* (stories of the second generation of women after the Sahabah, By Doctor Mustapaha Murad.

15- "Inspiration"-Your Ultimate Calling-Dr.W.W.Dyer.

16- Miracle of Life (a DVD-Video) by Lanneret Nilsson.

17- *Qisasil Anbiyah*(Stories of the Prophets) by, Imam Hafiz Ismael

18- Ibn Kathir

# Final Note

May this book serve as a radiant guide, inspiring each reader to honor and serve their parents with unwavering devotion. May we harness its wisdom to ascend in righteousness, secure Allah's pleasure, and ultimately enter the garden of everlasting reward beneath our mothers' feet.

All praise and thanks are due to Allah alone.

---

In the Name of Allah, the Most Gracious, the Most Merciful

O Allah, make us among those who preserve their prayers and perform them on time, and admit us through Baab As-Salah (The Gate of Prayer).

O Allah, strengthen us to strive in Your cause with our lives and wealth, and admit us through Baab Al-Jihad (The Gate of Striving).

O Allah, make us among those who fast sincerely and earnestly, and admit us through Baab Ar-Rayyan (The Gate of Fasting).

O Allah, bless us with a generous heart to give in Your path, and admit us through Baab As-Sadaqah (The Gate of Charity).

O Allah, ease for us the performance of Hajj with sincere intentions, and admit us through Baab Al-Hajj (The Gate of Pilgrimage).

O Allah, teach us patience in hardships, the restraint of anger, and forgiveness of others, and admit us through Baab Al-Kaazimeen Al-Ghaiz Wal Aafina Anin Naas (The Gate of Patience).

O Allah, forgive us for our sins and accept our repentance, and admit us through Baab At-Tawbah (The Gate of Repentance).

O Allah, let our tongues and hearts remain in constant remembrance of You, and admit us through Baab Al-Dhikr (The Gate of Remembrance of Allah).

Ya Allah, help us excel in these noble paths so all eight gates of Jannah may open for us. Let our lives be a testament to Your mercy and make us among those beloved to You in this world and the Hereafter.

Ameen, Ya Rabbal 'Alameen.

www.ingramcontent.com/pod-product-compliance
Lightning Source LLC
Chambersburg PA
CBHW052115030426
42335CB00025B/2988